Mastering PyTorch 2.6: Build, Train, and Deploy Neural Networks

Frances F. Thompson

Contents

Introduction

Welcome, fellow deep learning enthusiast! If you've picked up this book, chances are you're either curious about PyTorch, already dabbling in it, or perhaps even looking to level up your existing skills. No matter where you are on your journey, I'm thrilled to have you along for the ride. This book is your comprehensive guide to mastering PyTorch 2.6 and building, training, and deploying powerful neural networks.

• Target Audience and Book Overview

So, who is this book for? It's designed for individuals with a solid foundation in Python and a basic understanding of machine learning concepts. If you're comfortable with concepts like linear regression, classification, and basic neural networks, you're in the perfect spot. We're not going to rehash the fundamentals of machine learning; instead, we'll dive deep into how to implement those concepts effectively using PyTorch 2.6.

This isn't just another theory-heavy textbook. It's a hands-on guide packed with code examples, real-world applications, and best practices. We'll cover everything from tensor manipulation and custom layer creation to advanced optimization techniques and model deployment strategies. By the end of this book, you'll be able to:

- Build and train a wide variety of neural network architectures.
- Optimize your models for speed and efficiency using torch.compile.
- Deploy your models to production environments.
- Tackle challenging deep learning problems with confidence.

Think of this book as your mentor, guiding you through the complexities of PyTorch with clear explanations, practical examples, and a healthy dose of encouragement.

• Why PyTorch?

In the ever-evolving landscape of deep learning frameworks, why choose PyTorch? There are several compelling reasons:

- **Dynamic Computational Graphs:** PyTorch's dynamic graph approach offers incredible flexibility and ease of debugging. Unlike static graph frameworks, you can modify your model's architecture on the fly, making experimentation much faster and more intuitive. This is *huge* when you're trying out new ideas and need to iterate quickly.

- **Pythonic:** PyTorch feels natural to Python developers. It integrates seamlessly with the Python ecosystem, allowing you to leverage your existing skills and libraries. If you know Python, you'll feel right at home with PyTorch.
- **Large and Active Community:** PyTorch has a vibrant and supportive community. You'll find a wealth of resources, tutorials, and pre-trained models online. Getting stuck is inevitable in deep learning, but with the PyTorch community, you're never truly alone.
- **Production-Ready:** While PyTorch has always been strong in research, it's now fully equipped for production deployment, especially with tools like TorchScript and ONNX. You can build and train your models in PyTorch and then deploy them to a wide range of platforms.
- **torch.compile (Dynamo):** The game changer in PyTorch 2.x. This feature provides HUGE performance improvements out of the box with minimal code changes. We'll dedicate a whole chapter to mastering torch.compile because it's THAT important.

Personal Insight: I remember when I first started using PyTorch, I was blown away by how easy it was to experiment with different architectures. The dynamic graphs made debugging a breeze, and the Pythonic nature of the framework just felt natural. It truly accelerated my learning process.

• Setting Up Your Environment

Before we dive into the code, let's make sure you have a working PyTorch environment. I recommend using Anaconda or Miniconda to manage your Python environment. This will help you avoid dependency conflicts and keep your projects organized.

Here's a step-by-step guide:

1. **Install Anaconda or Miniconda:** Download and install the appropriate version for your operating system from the Anaconda website (https://www.anaconda.com/) or the Miniconda website (https://docs.conda.io/en/latest/miniconda.html).
2. **Create a New Environment:** Open your terminal or Anaconda Prompt and run the following command to create a new environment:

```
conda create -n pytorch_env python=3.9  # Or a Python
version you prefer
```

3. **Activate the Environment:**

```
conda activate pytorch_env
```

4. **Install PyTorch:** The installation command will vary depending on your operating system and whether you have a CUDA-enabled GPU. Visit the PyTorch website (https://pytorch.org/get-started/locally/) and select your configuration to generate the appropriate command. For example, a typical installation command might look like this:

```
conda install pytorch torchvision torchaudio pytorch-
cuda=11.6 -c pytorch -c nvidia
```

Important: Make sure you install the correct CUDA version to match your GPU. If you don't have a GPU, you can omit the pytorch-cuda dependency.

5. **Verify the Installation:** Once the installation is complete, open a Python interpreter within your activated environment and run the following code:

```
import torch
print(torch.__version__)
print(torch.cuda.is_available())  # Check if CUDA is
available
```

This should print the PyTorch version and True if CUDA is available (if you installed the CUDA version).

If everything is set up correctly, you're ready to start exploring the exciting world of PyTorch!

Personal Insight: I always recommend creating a separate environment for each of your deep learning projects. This helps prevent dependency conflicts and ensures that your projects are reproducible. Trust me, it will save you headaches down the road.

What's Next?

In the following chapters, we'll delve into the core concepts of PyTorch, starting with tensors and automatic differentiation. We'll then move on to building and training neural networks, exploring various architectures and optimization techniques. Finally, we'll cover deployment strategies and advanced topics like torch.compile and distributed training.

Get ready to roll up your sleeves and get your hands dirty with code! I'm excited to guide you on this journey to mastering PyTorch 2.6. Let's get started!

Part I: PyTorch Fundamentals

Chapter 1: Core Concepts

Welcome to Chapter 1! In this chapter, we'll lay the foundation for your PyTorch journey by exploring the three core concepts that underpin everything else: Tensors, Autograd, and the essential modules that make PyTorch so powerful. Think of this chapter as your toolbox—we're going to fill it with the essential tools you'll need to build amazing things.

1.1 Understanding Tensors: Data Types, Creation, and Manipulation

Tensors are the bedrock of PyTorch. Think of them as souped-up NumPy arrays designed for numerical computation and hardware acceleration. They're the containers for all your data, model weights, and gradients. So, getting comfortable with them is absolutely essential.

Why Tensors Matter: Forget manually tracking gradients or dealing with slow computations. Tensors, combined with PyTorch's automatic differentiation engine (which we'll cover later), make deep learning development faster and more intuitive.

Data Types: Choosing the Right Tool for the Job

PyTorch provides a rich set of data types for tensors. The choice depends on your needs for precision, memory efficiency, and hardware compatibility. Here's a quick guide to the most common ones:

Data Type	Description	Use Cases
torch.float32	32-bit floating-point (default)	General-purpose, good balance of precision and performance.
torch.float64	64-bit floating-point (double precision)	Applications requiring high precision, but at the cost of speed and memory.
torch.float16	16-bit floating-point (half precision)	Reducing memory footprint; often used with mixed-precision training.
torch.int64	64-bit integer	Indexing, counters, and representing discrete values.
torch.int32	32-bit integer	Similar to int64, but uses less memory.

torch.int8	8-bit integer	Quantization, representing pixel values in images.
torch.uint8	8-bit unsigned integer	Representing pixel values in images.
torch.bool	Boolean (True or False)	Masking, logical operations.

Personal Insight: I've found that torch.float32 strikes a good balance for most tasks. However, I've had success using torch.float16 with mixed-precision training to accelerate training and reduce memory usage, especially on GPUs with limited memory. It's definitely worth experimenting with!

Creating Tensors: From Data to PyTorch Powerhouse

Let's explore the different ways to create tensors. PyTorch offers several convenient functions:

```python
import torch
import numpy as np

# From a Python list
data = [1, 2, 3, 4, 5]
tensor_from_list = torch.tensor(data)
print(f"Tensor from list: {tensor_from_list}")

# From a NumPy array (copying data)
numpy_array = np.array([[1, 2], [3, 4]])
tensor_from_numpy = torch.tensor(numpy_array)
print(f"Tensor from NumPy array
(copied):\n{tensor_from_numpy}")

# From a NumPy array (sharing memory)
numpy_array = np.array([[1, 2], [3, 4]])
tensor_from_numpy_shared = torch.from_numpy(numpy_array)
print(f"Tensor from NumPy array (shared
memory):\n{tensor_from_numpy_shared}")

# Creating tensors with specific shapes and values
zeros_tensor = torch.zeros((2, 3))  # 2x3 tensor filled with
zeros
ones_tensor = torch.ones((3, 2))   # 3x2 tensor filled with
ones
random_tensor = torch.rand((2, 2))   # 2x2 tensor filled with
random numbers (0-1)
identity_matrix = torch.eye(3) #3x3 identity matrix

print(f"Zeros tensor:\n{zeros_tensor}")
print(f"Ones tensor:\n{ones_tensor}")
```

```
print(f"Random tensor:\n{random_tensor}")
print(f"Identity Matrix:\n{identity_matrix}")

# Creating a tensor with a specific data type
int_tensor = torch.tensor([1, 2, 3], dtype=torch.int32)
print(f"Integer tensor: {int_tensor.dtype}")
```

Key Differences: torch.tensor() *always* creates a new tensor, copying the data if needed. torch.from_numpy(), on the other hand, attempts to share the memory with the NumPy array. This can be much faster, but be mindful of potential side effects if you modify one.

Manipulating Tensors: Reshaping, Indexing, and Slicing

Once you have your tensors, you'll need to manipulate them to prepare your data for your neural network. PyTorch provides a powerful set of tools for reshaping, indexing, and slicing tensors.

```
    # Reshaping
original_tensor = torch.arange(12)   # Create a tensor with
values 0 to 11
reshaped_tensor = original_tensor.reshape((3, 4)) #Reshaping
to a 3x4 matrix
print(f"Original tensor: {original_tensor}")
print(f"Reshaped tensor:\n{reshaped_tensor}")

# Another way to reshape using view:
viewed_tensor = original_tensor.view(3, 4)
print(f"Viewed Tensor:\n{viewed_tensor}")

# Indexing and Slicing
subset = reshaped_tensor[0:2, 1:3] #Selecting rows 0 and 1,
and columns 1 and 2
print(f"Subset:\n{subset}")

# Transposing
transposed_tensor = reshaped_tensor.T # Transposing the
tensor
print(f"Transposed Tensor:\n{transposed_tensor}")

# Flattening: converts to 1D array
flattened_tensor = reshaped_tensor.flatten()
print(f"Flattened Tensor:\n{flattened_tensor}")
```

reshape vs. view: Both functions reshape a tensor, but view requires the new shape to be compatible with the original tensor's storage (i.e., the total number of elements must remain the same). reshape might copy the data if necessary to create a contiguous tensor in the desired shape. In most cases, view is more efficient when possible.

Mathematical Operations: Powering Your Neural Networks

Tensors support a wide range of mathematical operations, including element-wise addition, multiplication, matrix multiplication, and more.

```python
tensor_a = torch.tensor([[1, 2], [3, 4]],
dtype=torch.float32)
tensor_b = torch.tensor([[5, 6], [7, 8]],
dtype=torch.float32)

addition = tensor_a + tensor_b          # Element-wise addition
subtraction = tensor_a - tensor_b       # Element-wise
subtraction
multiplication = tensor_a * tensor_b  # Element-wise
multiplication
division = tensor_a / tensor_b          # Element-wise division
matrix_multiply = torch.matmul(tensor_a, tensor_b) # Matrix
multiplication

print(f"Addition:\n{addition}")
print(f"Subtraction:\n{subtraction}")
print(f"Multiplication:\n{multiplication}")
print(f"Division:\n{division}")
print(f"Matrix Multiply:\n{matrix_multiply}")

# Exponentiation
exponentiated_tensor = torch.exp(tensor_a)
print(f"Exponentiated Tensor:\n{exponentiated_tensor}")
```

Moving Tensors to the GPU: Unleashing the Power

To leverage the power of GPUs for accelerated computation, you need to move your tensors to the GPU. Here's how:

```python
if torch.cuda.is_available():
    device = torch.device("cuda")  # Use "cuda:0" if you have
multiple GPUs
    tensor_gpu = tensor_a.to(device) # Copies tensor_a to the
GPU
```

```
    print(f"Tensor on GPU: {tensor_gpu}")
else:
    print("CUDA is not available. Running on CPU.")
```

Best Practice: Always check torch.cuda.is_available() before attempting to move tensors to the GPU. If CUDA isn't available, your code will crash.

Conclusion

You've now gained a solid understanding of PyTorch tensors, covering data types, creation, manipulation, mathematical operations, and GPU acceleration. These skills will be invaluable as you build more complex neural networks. In the next section, we'll delve into Autograd, the engine that makes automatic differentiation possible.

1.2 Autograd: Automatic Differentiation Explained

One of the most magical, and arguably *most* important features of PyTorch is **Autograd**, short for Automatic Differentiation. If you've ever manually calculated the derivative of a complex function, you'll immediately understand why this is a game-changer. Autograd automates the process of computing gradients (derivatives) of tensor operations, which is absolutely crucial for training neural networks using gradient descent.

Why Autograd Matters: In essence, it frees you from the tedious and error-prone task of manually calculating gradients. This allows you to focus on designing your neural network architecture and experimenting with different loss functions, knowing that PyTorch will handle the gradient computations behind the scenes.

Understanding Computational Graphs: The Key to Automatic Differentiation

Autograd works by building a *computational graph* that meticulously tracks all the operations performed on tensors. Think of it as a recipe that PyTorch creates as you perform calculations. When you call backward() on a tensor, PyTorch traverses this graph *in reverse*, applying the chain rule to compute the gradients of each operation with respect to the input tensors.

Let's illustrate this with a simple example:

```
    import torch

# Create a tensor and tell PyTorch to track its gradient
x = torch.tensor(2.0, requires_grad=True)

# Define a simple function: y = x^2 + 2x + 1
y = x**2 + 2*x + 1

# Compute the gradient of y with respect to x
y.backward()

# Print the computed gradient (dy/dx at x=2)
print(x.grad)   # Output: tensor(6.)
```

Let's break down what's happening in the code:

1. **requires_grad=True:** This is the magic ingredient! It tells PyTorch to track all operations performed on the tensor x so it can calculate gradients later. If you forget this, Autograd won't work.
2. **y = x**2 + 2*x + 1:** This defines a simple mathematical function. PyTorch builds a computational graph representing this function.
3. **y.backward():** This triggers the automatic differentiation process. PyTorch traverses the computational graph in reverse, calculating the gradient of y with respect to x (dy/dx).
4. **x.grad:** This accesses the computed gradient, which is stored in the grad attribute of the x tensor. The value 6.0 is the derivative of $y = x^2 + 2x + 1$ evaluated at $x = 2$. $(2x + 2 = 22 + 2 = 6)$

Personal Insight: I remember the first time I used Autograd, I was amazed by how simple it made the process of training neural networks. No more manually calculating gradients – PyTorch handled it all! It truly freed me up to focus on the more creative aspects of deep learning.

Controlling Autograd: When and How to Turn it Off

While Autograd is incredibly useful for training, there are situations where you don't want PyTorch to track operations. This is especially true during inference (when you're using a trained model to make predictions) or when performing operations that don't require gradients. Tracking gradients consumes memory and computational resources, so disabling Autograd can significantly improve performance.

There are two main ways to control Autograd:

1. **torch.no_grad() Context Manager:** This is the preferred way to temporarily disable Autograd. Any operations performed within the torch.no_grad() block will not be tracked.

```
    x = torch.tensor(2.0, requires_grad=True)

with torch.no_grad():
    y = x**2 + 2*x + 1   # Operations within this block are
not tracked

print(y)   # Output: tensor(9.) - No gradient computed.

#Attempting to call y.backward() here would raise an error.
```

2. **detach() Method:** This method creates a new tensor that shares the same data as the original tensor but *doesn't* require gradient computation. Detaching a tensor effectively breaks the connection to the computational graph.

```
    x = torch.tensor(2.0, requires_grad=True)

# Detach x from the computation graph
x_detached = x.detach()

# Perform operations with the detached tensor
y = x_detached**2 + 2*x_detached + 1

print(y)   # Output: tensor(9.) - No gradient computed.

# Attempting to call y.backward() here would raise an error.
```

When to Use Which: Use torch.no_grad() when you want to perform several operations without tracking gradients, such as during inference. Use detach() when you need to break the connection to the computational graph for a specific tensor, often when manipulating data between the generator and discriminator in GANs.

A More Complex Example: Backpropagation in a Simple Neural Network

Let's solidify your understanding with a more complex example: backpropagation in a simple neural network. This example will demonstrate how Autograd works behind the scenes to update the model's weights.

```python
import torch
import torch.nn as nn

# Define a simple linear layer
linear_layer = nn.Linear(in_features=10, out_features=1)

# Create some random input data
x = torch.randn(1, 10)   # Batch size of 1, input size of 10

# Perform a forward pass
y_predicted = linear_layer(x)

# Define a target value
y_target = torch.tensor([[1.0]])

# Define a loss function (mean squared error)
loss_fn = nn.MSELoss()
loss = loss_fn(y_predicted, y_target)

# Print the initial loss
print(f"Initial loss: {loss.item()}")

# Perform backpropagation
loss.backward()

# Update the model's weights
learning_rate = 0.01
with torch.no_grad():
    for param in linear_layer.parameters():
        param.data -= learning_rate * param.grad

# Zero the gradients (important for the next iteration!)
linear_layer.zero_grad()

# Perform another forward pass and print the updated loss
y_predicted = linear_layer(x)
loss = loss_fn(y_predicted, y_target)
print(f"Updated loss: {loss.item()}")
```

In this example, Autograd automatically calculates the gradients of the loss function with respect to the model's weights. We then use these gradients to update the weights and reduce the loss. Notice that we use torch.no_grad() when updating the weights to prevent Autograd from tracking these operations.

Conclusion

You now have a solid grasp of Autograd, one of the most powerful features of PyTorch. By understanding how Autograd works and how to control it, you can efficiently train complex neural networks and experiment with different architectures and loss functions. In the next section, we'll explore the essential PyTorch modules that provide the building blocks for creating and training neural networks.

1.3 Essential Modules: nn, optim, data, and Utilities - Your PyTorch Toolkit

Now that we've covered the fundamental concepts of Tensors and Autograd, it's time to explore the essential modules that make PyTorch so powerful and user-friendly. These modules provide the building blocks for creating, training, and deploying neural networks with ease. Think of this as stocking your deep learning toolkit with the instruments you'll use daily.

Why These Modules Matter: These modules abstract away much of the low-level complexity, allowing you to focus on designing your models and solving your problems. They provide a consistent and well-designed API that makes PyTorch a joy to use.

torch.nn: Building Blocks for Neural Networks

The torch.nn module is the heart of PyTorch when it comes to defining neural network architectures. It provides a vast collection of pre-built layers, activation functions, and other components that you can use to assemble your models.

Key Concepts:

- **Layers:** Fundamental building blocks like linear layers (nn.Linear), convolutional layers (nn.Conv2d), recurrent layers (nn.LSTM, nn.GRU), and more.
- **Activation Functions:** Non-linear functions like ReLU (nn.ReLU), Sigmoid (nn.Sigmoid), Tanh (nn.Tanh), and others that introduce non-linearity into your models.
- **Containers:** Modules like nn.Sequential (for creating linear stacks of layers) and nn.ModuleList (for managing lists of modules).
- **Loss Functions:** Criteria for evaluating the performance of the model, such as nn.MSELoss (Mean Squared Error), nn.CrossEntropyLoss (for classification), and others.

Personal Insight: The nn module is where you'll spend most of your time when defining your neural network architectures. It's worth taking the time to explore the available layers and understand their functionality. I often refer to the PyTorch documentation to find the right layer for the job.

Let's illustrate this with an example:

```python
import torch
import torch.nn as nn
import torch.nn.functional as F  # For functional (stateless)
components

# Define a simple feedforward neural network
class SimpleNet(nn.Module):
    def __init__(self, input_size, hidden_size, output_size):
        super(SimpleNet, self).__init__()
        self.fc1 = nn.Linear(input_size, hidden_size)  #
Fully connected layer 1
        self.relu = nn.ReLU()                          # ReLU
activation
        self.fc2 = nn.Linear(hidden_size, output_size) #
Fully connected layer 2

    def forward(self, x):
        x = self.fc1(x)  # Pass input through fully connected
layer 1
        x = self.relu(x) # Apply ReLU activation
        x = self.fc2(x)  # Pass through fully connected layer
2
        return x

# Instantiate the model
input_size = 10
hidden_size = 5
output_size = 1
model = SimpleNet(input_size, hidden_size, output_size)

# Print the model architecture
print(model)
```

In this example, we define a simple feedforward neural network using nn.Module. The __init__ method defines the layers of the network, and the forward method defines the flow of data through the network.

torch.optim: Training Your Models with Optimization Algorithms

The torch.optim module provides a collection of optimization algorithms for training your neural networks. These algorithms are used to update the model's weights based on the gradients computed by Autograd.

Key Concepts:

- **Optimization Algorithms:** Popular algorithms like Stochastic Gradient Descent (SGD), Adam, RMSprop, and others.
- **Learning Rate Schedulers:** Techniques for adjusting the learning rate during training to improve convergence and performance.

```python
import torch.optim as optim

# Define an optimizer (Adam is a popular choice)
learning_rate = 0.001
optimizer = optim.Adam(model.parameters(), lr=learning_rate)
```

In this example, we create an Adam optimizer that will update the weights of the model based on the gradients computed during backpropagation. The lr parameter specifies the learning rate.

Personal Insight: Choosing the right optimizer and tuning the learning rate are crucial for successful training. I often experiment with different optimizers and learning rate schedules to find the best configuration for my models.

torch.utils.data: Loading and Preprocessing Data

The torch.utils.data module provides tools for loading and preprocessing data, making it easier to work with large datasets.

Key Concepts:

- **Dataset:** An abstract class that represents a dataset. You'll typically subclass this class to create your own custom datasets.
- **DataLoader:** A class that iterates over a dataset in batches, providing a convenient way to load data during training.

```python
import torch
from torch.utils.data import Dataset, DataLoader

# Example: A simple custom dataset
class MyDataset(Dataset):
```

```
    def __init__(self, data, labels):
        self.data = torch.tensor(data, dtype=torch.float32)
        self.labels = torch.tensor(labels,
dtype=torch.float32)

    def __len__(self):
        return len(self.data)

    def __getitem__(self, idx):
        return self.data[idx], self.labels[idx]


# Sample data
data = [[1, 2, 3, 4, 5, 6, 7, 8, 9, 10],
        [11, 12, 13, 14, 15, 16, 17, 18, 19, 20],
        [21, 22, 23, 24, 25, 26, 27, 28, 29, 30]]  # Input
size is 10
labels = [1, 0, 1]  # Sample labels

# Instantiate the dataset
dataset = MyDataset(data, labels)

# Instantiate the data loader
batch_size = 2
dataloader = DataLoader(dataset, batch_size=batch_size,
shuffle=True) # shuffle data each epoch

# Iterate over the data loader
for batch_idx, (data, labels) in enumerate(dataloader):
    print(f"Batch {batch_idx + 1}:")
    print(f"  Data: {data}")
    print(f"  Labels: {labels}")

    # At this point you would pass the data to the model
    # and train it with the labels
    # break #Remove break after testing
    break # For the purpose of this example, we only show one
batch
```

In this example, we create a custom dataset called MyDataset that loads data and labels from NumPy arrays. We then create a DataLoader that iterates over the dataset in batches. The shuffle=True argument shuffles the data at the beginning of each epoch (iteration over the entire dataset).

Other Useful Utilities

PyTorch provides a number of other useful utilities that can simplify your deep learning workflow. Some notable examples include:

- **torch.nn.functional (often aliased as F):** Contains functional versions of many nn layers and other functions (e.g., activation functions, loss functions) that don't have any internal state. This is often used when you need more control over how the operations are performed.
- **torch.cuda:** For managing GPU devices and memory. This allows you to move tensors and models to the GPU for accelerated computation.
- **torch.save and torch.load:** For saving and loading trained models.

Personal Insight: I frequently use torch.nn.functional for activation functions and loss functions when I need more flexibility. Also, mastering torch.cuda is essential for maximizing the performance of your models.

Conclusion

You've now explored the essential PyTorch modules: nn, optim, data, and other utilities. These modules provide the building blocks for creating, training, and deploying powerful neural networks. By mastering these modules, you'll be well-equipped to tackle a wide range of deep learning problems. In the next chapter, we'll start building and training more complex neural networks. Get ready to put your newfound knowledge into practice!

Chapter 2: Advanced Tensor Operations - Unleashing Tensor Power

Welcome back! In this chapter, we'll delve into advanced tensor operations, equipping you with the skills to manipulate tensors efficiently and effectively. We'll move beyond the basics and explore techniques that are crucial for building complex neural networks and optimizing your code for performance. Think of this chapter as learning advanced techniques in the kitchen to make the most out of your ingredients.

Why Advanced Tensor Operations Matter: Mastering these techniques will allow you to write more concise, efficient, and scalable code. You'll be able to handle larger datasets, build more complex models, and take full advantage of the hardware acceleration offered by PyTorch.

2.1 Broadcasting and Vectorization Techniques: Simplifying Operations

In the realm of PyTorch, *broadcasting* and *vectorization* are your secret weapons for writing concise and blazing-fast code. They allow you to perform operations on tensors of different shapes without writing explicit loops, leading to both cleaner syntax and significant performance improvements. Think of it as having a magic wand that makes complex operations effortless.

Why Broadcasting and Vectorization Matter: Manually looping through tensors element by element is slow and cumbersome. Broadcasting and vectorization leverage optimized low-level implementations, allowing you to perform operations on entire tensors simultaneously, maximizing your CPU or GPU's processing capabilities. They're *essential* for efficient deep learning.

Broadcasting: Adapting Tensor Shapes

Broadcasting is a set of rules that govern how PyTorch handles operations between tensors with different shapes. Instead of throwing an error when you try to add or multiply tensors with incompatible dimensions, PyTorch attempts to *broadcast* one or both tensors to make them compatible.

Let's illustrate with code:

```python
import torch

# Example 1: Adding a scalar to a tensor
tensor_a = torch.tensor([1, 2, 3])
scalar = 2
result = tensor_a + scalar  # Broadcasting the scalar to
match tensor_a's shape
print(f"Adding a scalar:\n{result}")

# Example 2: Adding a 1D tensor to a 2D tensor
tensor_b = torch.tensor([[1, 2, 3], [4, 5, 6]])
tensor_c = torch.tensor([10, 20, 30])
result = tensor_b + tensor_c  # Broadcasting tensor_c to
match tensor_b's shape
print(f"Adding a 1D tensor to a 2D tensor:\n{result}")

# Example 3: Comparing two tensors of different shapes
tensor_d = torch.tensor([[1, 2, 3], [4, 5, 6]])
tensor_e = torch.tensor([2, 4, 2])
result = tensor_d > tensor_e
print(f"Comparison of two tensors:\n{result}")
```

Personal Insight: The first time I encountered broadcasting, I was initially confused. But once I understood the underlying rules, it became an indispensable tool for simplifying my code. It's like having a built-in shape adapter for your tensors.

The Broadcasting Rules:

To understand how broadcasting works, let's break down the rules:

1. **Rank Alignment:** If the tensors don't have the same number of dimensions (rank), PyTorch prepends dimensions of size 1 to the tensor with the lower rank until both tensors have the same number of dimensions. For example, a tensor with shape (3,) would be treated as if it had shape (1, 3) before any operation is performed.
2. **Dimension Compatibility:** Two dimensions are compatible if:
   o   They are equal in size, or
   o   One of them is 1.
3. **Broadcasting Eligibility:** The tensors can be broadcast together if they are compatible in *all* dimensions.

4. **The Broadcasted Shape:** After broadcasting, each tensor behaves as if it had a shape equal to the element-wise maximum of the shapes of the two input tensors.
5. **Expansion of Size 1 Dimensions:** In any dimension where one tensor has size 1 and the other tensor has a size greater than 1, the first tensor is virtually copied along that dimension as many times as needed to match the size of the second tensor.

Vectorization: Unleashing SIMD Power

Vectorization is the technique of performing operations on entire arrays or tensors simultaneously, rather than element-by-element. This leverages SIMD (Single Instruction, Multiple Data) instructions, which allow the CPU or GPU to perform the same operation on multiple data points in parallel.

Why Vectorization is Fast: Modern processors are designed to perform vectorized operations efficiently. By using vectorized code, you're essentially telling the processor to use its specialized hardware for parallel computation, resulting in significant speedups.

Let's revisit our previous examples, but this time with a focus on how vectorization is implicitly being used:

```python
import torch

# Example 1: Element-wise addition
tensor_a = torch.tensor([1, 2, 3, 4, 5])
tensor_b = torch.tensor([6, 7, 8, 9, 10])

result = tensor_a + tensor_b  # Vectorized addition
print(f"Vectorized Addition:\n{result}")

# Example 2: Element-wise multiplication
tensor_c = torch.tensor([[1, 2], [3, 4]])
tensor_d = torch.tensor([[5, 6], [7, 8]])

result = tensor_c * tensor_d # Vectorized multiplication
print(f"Vectorized Multiplication:\n{result}")
```

Behind the Scenes: When you perform tensor_a + tensor_b, PyTorch doesn't iterate through the tensors element by element. Instead, it calls highly optimized functions from libraries like BLAS (Basic Linear Algebra Subprograms) that are specifically designed for vectorized operations.

Combining Broadcasting and Vectorization: A Powerful Duo

Broadcasting and vectorization often work together to simplify operations and improve performance. Broadcasting allows you to perform operations on tensors with different shapes, while vectorization ensures that those operations are performed efficiently.

```python
import torch

# Example: Subtracting the mean from each row of a matrix
tensor_a = torch.tensor([[1, 2, 3], [4, 5, 6]],
dtype=torch.float32)
row_means = torch.mean(tensor_a, dim=1, keepdim=True) #
Calculate the mean of each row. Keep dimensions so it can be
broadcasted correctly.

result = tensor_a - row_means  # Broadcasting and
vectorization
print(f"Subtracting Row Means:\n{result}")
```

In this example, we first calculate the mean of each row of the tensor using torch.mean(tensor_a, dim=1, keepdim=True). The keepdim=True argument ensures that the row_means tensor has the same number of dimensions as tensor_a, allowing it to be broadcasted correctly. Then, we subtract the row_means from tensor_a, which is both a vectorized and broadcasted operation.

Common Pitfalls and Best Practices:

- **Memory Usage:** Be mindful of memory usage when broadcasting large tensors. Broadcasting creates virtual copies, but the memory is still allocated.
- **Explicit Broadcasting:** If you're unsure whether broadcasting will work as expected, you can explicitly broadcast tensors using torch.broadcast_to() to ensure compatibility.

```python
tensor_a = torch.tensor([1, 2, 3])
broadcasted_tensor = torch.broadcast_to(tensor_a, (2, 3))
print(f"Explicitly Broadcasted
Tensor:\n{broadcasted_tensor}")
```

Personal Insight: I've occasionally made mistakes when broadcasting tensors with complex shapes. Always double-check the shapes of your tensors and use torch.broadcast_to() if you're unsure.

Conclusion

Broadcasting and vectorization are essential techniques for writing efficient and concise PyTorch code. By understanding the broadcasting rules and leveraging vectorized operations, you can significantly improve the performance of your deep learning models. In the next section, we'll explore advanced indexing, slicing, and reshaping techniques.

2.2 Indexing, Slicing, and Reshaping for Efficiency: Accessing and Transforming Data

In the world of PyTorch, efficiently accessing and transforming your data is crucial for both performance and readability. Indexing, slicing, and reshaping are the tools that enable you to extract specific elements, create subsets, and change the structure of your tensors without unnecessary copying. Think of it as being able to precisely manipulate the ingredients you have so they can be perfectly used in your recipe.

Why Efficient Data Manipulation Matters: Poorly optimized data manipulation can become a bottleneck in your deep learning pipelines, especially when dealing with large datasets. Mastering these techniques will allow you to write code that is both fast and memory-efficient.

Indexing: Precise Access to Tensor Elements

Indexing allows you to access individual elements within a tensor using their numerical positions, or indices.

```python
import torch

# Create a 1D tensor
tensor_1d = torch.tensor([10, 20, 30, 40, 50])

# Accessing individual elements
first_element = tensor_1d[0]   # Access the element at index 0
print(f"First Element: {first_element}")

# Create a 2D tensor
tensor_2d = torch.tensor([[1, 2, 3], [4, 5, 6], [7, 8, 9]])
```

```
# Accessing elements in a 2D tensor
element_2_1 = tensor_2d[1, 0]   # Access the element at row 1,
column 0
print(f"Element at [1, 0]: {element_2_1}")

#Advanced indexing using tensors

index_tensor = torch.tensor([0, 2]) #Access index 0 and 2
from tensor_1d
selected_elements = tensor_1d[index_tensor]
print(f"Selected elements:\n{selected_elements}")
```

Personal Insight: When starting out, I found it helpful to visualize tensors as multi-dimensional grids. Remembering that indexing starts at 0 is key to avoiding off-by-one errors!

Slicing: Extracting Subsets of Tensors

Slicing allows you to extract a portion or "slice" of a tensor, creating a new tensor that contains a subset of the original data.

```
    import torch

# Create a 1D tensor
tensor_1d = torch.arange(10)   # Create a tensor with values
from 0 to 9
print(f"Original 1D Tensor: {tensor_1d}")

# Slicing a 1D tensor
subset_1d = tensor_1d[2:7]   # Select elements from index 2 up
to (but not including) 7
print(f"Subset of 1D Tensor: {subset_1d}")

# Create a 2D tensor
tensor_2d = torch.arange(20).reshape(4, 5)   # Create a 4x5
tensor
print(f"Original 2D Tensor:\n{tensor_2d}")

# Slicing a 2D tensor
subset_2d = tensor_2d[1:3, 2:4]   # Select rows 1 and 2, and
columns 2 and 3
print(f"Subset of 2D Tensor:\n{subset_2d}")

#Slicing every other element
subset_every_other = tensor_1d[::2]
print(f"Every other element of 1D
Tensor:\n{subset_every_other}")
```

```
#Using ... (Ellipsis) for slicing higher dimensions
tensor_3d = torch.randn(2, 3, 4, 5)
subset_ellipsis = tensor_3d[0, ..., 2] #Gets the first
"batch" then every element up to 2 on last dimension.
print(f"Shape of subset using Ellipsis:
{subset_ellipsis.shape}")
```

Key Concepts:

- The general syntax for slicing is tensor[start:stop:step].
- start is the index where the slice begins (inclusive).
- stop is the index where the slice ends (exclusive).
- step is the increment between indices (default is 1).
- Leaving start or stop blank implies the beginning or end of the tensor, respectively.

Reshaping: Changing Tensor Structure without Data Copying

Reshaping allows you to change the shape of a tensor without altering its underlying data. This is essential for preparing your data for different layers in your neural network.

```
import torch

# Create a tensor
tensor_a = torch.arange(12)   # Create a tensor with values
from 0 to 11
print(f"Original Tensor: {tensor_a}")

# Reshaping the tensor
reshaped_tensor = tensor_a.reshape(3, 4)   # Reshape to a 3x4
tensor
print(f"Reshaped Tensor:\n{reshaped_tensor}")

# Reshaping with view (preferred for efficiency)
viewed_tensor = tensor_a.view(3, 4)   # Same reshape, but
using view
print(f"Viewed Tensor:\n{viewed_tensor}")

# Inferring Dimension Size
inferred_shape = tensor_a.view(2, -1) #PyTorch infers the
size of the second dimension
print(f"Inferred shape Tensor:\n{inferred_shape}")

# Transposing
```

```
transposed_tensor = reshaped_tensor.T  # Transpose rows and
columns
print(f"Transposed Tensor:\n{transposed_tensor}")

# Flattening
flattened_tensor = reshaped_tensor.flatten()  # Converts the
tensor to 1D
print(f"Flattened Tensor:\n{flattened_tensor}")

#Adding a dimension:
unsqueeze_tensor = tensor_a.unsqueeze(dim=0) #Adds a
dimension at position 0
print(f"Unsqueezed Tensor: {unsqueeze_tensor.shape}")

#Removing a dimension:
squeezed_tensor = unsqueeze_tensor.squeeze() #Removes
dimension of size one.
print(f"Squeezed Tensor: {squeezed_tensor.shape}")
```

Key Differences: reshape vs. view

Both functions reshape a tensor, but view has some restrictions. view can
only be used if the new shape is *contiguous* with the original tensor's
memory layout. reshape will copy the data if necessary to create a
contiguous tensor, making it more flexible but potentially less efficient.

Personal Insight: I've learned to prefer view whenever possible, as it avoids
unnecessary data copying and can significantly improve performance.
However, it's important to be aware of the contiguity requirements.

Reshaping for Neural Networks:

Reshaping is particularly useful when preparing data for different layers in
your neural network. For example, you might need to flatten a convolutional
feature map before feeding it into a fully connected layer.

Common Pitfalls and Best Practices:

- **Contiguity:** Always be mindful of tensor contiguity when using
  view. If you're unsure whether a tensor is contiguous, you can use
  tensor.is_contiguous() to check.
- **Memory Usage:** Reshaping does not copy the data, so it's a very
  efficient operation.

- **Error Handling:** Be careful when specifying the new shape, as incorrect dimensions can lead to errors.

Conclusion

By mastering indexing, slicing, and reshaping, you can efficiently access and transform your data in PyTorch. These techniques are essential for writing code that is both fast and memory-efficient. You are now armed with the skills to skillfully access and prepare your data! In the next section, we will continue building our skills as we examine linear algebra.

2.3 Linear Algebra Operations: Dot Products, Matrix Multiplication, and Decompositions - The Foundation of Deep Learning

Linear algebra lies at the very core of deep learning. From the forward pass of a neural network to the optimization algorithms that update its weights, linear algebra operations are constantly being performed. In this section, we'll explore some of the most fundamental linear algebra operations in PyTorch, including dot products, matrix multiplication, and decompositions. Mastering these concepts is like learning the alphabet and basic grammar before writing a novel – it's *essential*.

Why Linear Algebra Matters: Without a solid understanding of linear algebra, you'll be limited in your ability to design, analyze, and optimize deep learning models. These operations are not just abstract mathematical concepts; they are the building blocks of everything you'll do in PyTorch.

Dot Products: Measuring Similarity

The dot product (also known as the inner product or scalar product) is a fundamental operation that measures the similarity between two vectors. It's calculated by multiplying corresponding elements of the vectors and then summing the results.

```
import torch

# Create two vectors
vector_a = torch.tensor([1, 2, 3], dtype=torch.float32)
vector_b = torch.tensor([4, 5, 6], dtype=torch.float32)

# Calculate the dot product
```

```
dot_product = torch.dot(vector_a, vector_b)
print(f"Dot Product: {dot_product}") #Output: 32.0
```

Interpretation: The dot product is large when the vectors are pointing in similar directions and small (or negative) when they are pointing in opposite directions. The magnitude of the dot product is related to the lengths of the vectors and the cosine of the angle between them.

Applications: Dot products are used in many deep learning applications, including:

- Calculating the similarity between word embeddings.
- Implementing attention mechanisms.
- Measuring the alignment between feature vectors.

Matrix Multiplication: Transforming Data Spaces

Matrix multiplication is a more general operation than the dot product that allows you to transform data from one space to another. In a neural network, matrix multiplication is used to apply weights to the input data and propagate it through the layers.

```
import torch

# Create two matrices
matrix_a = torch.tensor([[1, 2], [3, 4]],
dtype=torch.float32)
matrix_b = torch.tensor([[5, 6], [7, 8]],
dtype=torch.float32)

# Calculate the matrix product using torch.matmul
matrix_product = torch.matmul(matrix_a, matrix_b)
print(f"Matrix Product (matmul):\n{matrix_product}")

# Alternative using @ operator (syntactic sugar)
matrix_product_alt = matrix_a @ matrix_b
print(f"Matrix Product (@):\n{matrix_product_alt}")

#Batch Matrix Multiplication
tensor_c = torch.randn(3, 4, 5) #Batch size 3, 4x5 matrices
tensor_d = torch.randn(3, 5, 6) #Batch size 3, 5x6 matrices

batch_matrix_multiply = torch.bmm(tensor_c, tensor_d) #Batch
matrix multiply
print(f"Batch Matrix Multiply shape:
{batch_matrix_multiply.shape}") #Should be [3,4,6]
```

Understanding Dimensions:

- If matrix_a has shape (m, n) and matrix_b has shape (n, p), then matrix_product will have shape (m, p).
- The number of columns in matrix_a must equal the number of rows in matrix_b.

Personal Insight: I think of matrix multiplication as a way to "mix" the information in two matrices. The resulting matrix contains a combination of the features present in both input matrices.

Applications: Matrix multiplication is ubiquitous in deep learning and is used for:

- Linear transformations in fully connected layers.
- Convolutions in convolutional neural networks.
- Recurrent operations in recurrent neural networks.

Matrix Decompositions: Unveiling Hidden Structures

Matrix decompositions are a set of techniques for breaking down a matrix into its constituent parts, revealing hidden structures and properties. PyTorch supports a variety of matrix decompositions, including singular value decomposition (SVD), eigenvalue decomposition, and more.

```
    import torch

# Create a matrix
matrix_a = torch.tensor([[1, 2], [3, 4]],
dtype=torch.float32)

# Singular Value Decomposition (SVD)
U, S, V = torch.linalg.svd(matrix_a)
print(f"U:\n{U}")
print(f"S:\n{S}")
print(f"V:\n{V}")

#Reconstructing original Matrix
reconstructed_matrix = U @ torch.diag(S) @ V.T
print(f"Reconstructed matrix:\n{reconstructed_matrix}")
```

Understanding SVD:

- SVD decomposes a matrix into three matrices: U, S, and V.
- U and V are orthogonal matrices, and S is a diagonal matrix containing the singular values.
- The singular values represent the importance of different dimensions in the original matrix.

Applications: Matrix decompositions have a wide range of applications, including:

- Dimensionality reduction (e.g., Principal Component Analysis - PCA).
- Image compression.
- Recommender systems.
- Solving linear systems of equations.

Personal Insight: I've used SVD for dimensionality reduction in several projects, and it can be a powerful tool for simplifying complex datasets and improving model performance.

Choosing the Right Operation:

- Use torch.dot() for the dot product of two 1D tensors (vectors).
- Use torch.matmul() or the @ operator for matrix multiplication. torch.matmul also handles broadcasting in certain scenarios.
- Use torch.linalg.svd() for singular value decomposition. Other decompositions are available in torch.linalg.

Conclusion

You've now gained a solid understanding of fundamental linear algebra operations in PyTorch, including dot products, matrix multiplication, and decompositions. These operations are the foundation of deep learning, and mastering them will enable you to build and analyze more complex models. In the next section, we'll explore how to work with sparse tensors, which are essential for handling data with high sparsity.

2.4 Working with Sparse Tensors: Handling Data Sparsity - Efficiency in a World of Zeros

In many real-world datasets, a significant portion of the data consists of zeros. This phenomenon is known as *sparsity*. Storing and processing these datasets using dense tensors can be highly inefficient, wasting memory and computational resources. That's where sparse tensors come to the rescue! They are specifically designed to represent and manipulate data with high sparsity, offering substantial savings in memory and performance. Think of it as packing only what you need for a trip, leaving the extra baggage behind.

Why Sparse Tensors Matter: As you work with larger datasets, particularly in areas like natural language processing, recommender systems, and graph analysis, sparsity becomes increasingly common. Using sparse tensors allows you to handle these datasets effectively and efficiently.

Understanding Sparsity: The Prevalence of Zeros

Sparsity refers to the proportion of zero elements in a tensor. A tensor is considered sparse if a significant fraction of its elements are zero. For example, a one-hot encoded vector representing a word in a vocabulary is often very sparse, as only one element (corresponding to the present word) is non-zero.

Types of Sparse Data:

- **One-Hot Encoded Vectors:** Used to represent categorical variables.
- **Document-Term Matrices:** Represent the frequency of words in a collection of documents.
- **Adjacency Matrices for Graphs:** Represent the connections between nodes in a graph.
- **Recommender System Data:** User-item interaction matrices, where most users have interacted with only a small fraction of the available items.

Sparse Tensor Formats: Storing Non-Zero Elements

Sparse tensors store only the non-zero elements and their corresponding indices, significantly reducing memory usage compared to dense tensors. PyTorch supports several sparse tensor formats, each with its own advantages and disadvantages.

- **COO (Coordinate) Format:** Stores the coordinates (indices) and values of the non-zero elements. This is a simple and versatile format that is suitable for many applications.
- **CSR (Compressed Sparse Row) and CSC (Compressed Sparse Column) Formats:** Optimized for matrix-vector multiplication. CSR

is efficient for row-wise operations, while CSC is efficient for column-wise operations.
- **BCOO (Block Coordinate) Format:** An extension of COO that stores non-zero blocks of elements. Useful when there are structures in your data.

Personal Insight: I've found the COO format to be a good starting point for working with sparse tensors, as it's relatively simple to understand and use. However, for performance-critical applications, it's worth exploring CSR or CSC, especially if you're performing frequent matrix-vector multiplications.

Creating and Manipulating Sparse Tensors in PyTorch

Let's dive into the code and see how to create and manipulate sparse tensors in PyTorch.

```python
import torch

# 1. Creating a sparse tensor from a dense tensor (COO
Format)
dense_tensor = torch.tensor([[0, 0, 1, 0],
                             [0, 2, 0, 0],
                             [3, 0, 0, 4]])

sparse_tensor_coo = dense_tensor.to_sparse_coo() # Create
sparse COO tensor

print(f"Sparse COO Tensor:\n{sparse_tensor_coo}") # Prints
the indices and values

# 2. Creating a sparse tensor directly (COO Format)
indices = torch.tensor([[0, 2], # Index for value of 1
                        [1, 1], # Index for value of 2
                        [2, 0], # Index for value of 3
                        [2, 3]]) # Index for value of 4
values = torch.tensor([1, 2, 3, 4], dtype=torch.float32)

sparse_tensor_direct = torch.sparse_coo_tensor(indices.T,
values, dense_tensor.size())  # Sizes must match

print(f"Sparse Tensor (Direct
Creation):\n{sparse_tensor_direct}")

# 3. Converting back to dense tensor
dense_tensor_reconstructed = sparse_tensor_coo.to_dense()
print(f"Reconstructed Dense
Tensor:\n{dense_tensor_reconstructed}")
```

```
# 4. Basic operations - Element wise addition

sparse_tensor_a = torch.sparse_coo_tensor(torch.tensor([[0,
1], [1, 0]]).T, torch.tensor([1, 2], dtype=torch.float32),
(2, 2))
sparse_tensor_b = torch.sparse_coo_tensor(torch.tensor([[0,
0], [1, 1]]).T, torch.tensor([3, 4], dtype=torch.float32),
(2, 2))

sparse_sum = sparse_tensor_a + sparse_tensor_b
print(f"Sparse Sum:\n{sparse_sum.to_dense()}") # Needs to be
converted to dense to visualize
```

Key Observations:

- indices: This tensor stores the coordinates of the non-zero elements. Each column of the indices tensor represents the coordinates of a non-zero element.
- values: This tensor stores the values of the non-zero elements, corresponding to the coordinates specified in the indices tensor.
- dense_shape: This argument specifies the shape of the dense tensor that the sparse tensor represents.

Important Notes:

- The indices must be sorted in lexicographical order (row-major order).
- The shape of the dense tensor must be provided when creating a sparse tensor directly.
- PyTorch supports limited operations directly on sparse tensors. Often, you'll need to convert them to dense tensors for certain operations.

Working with Sparse Matrices

```
import torch

# Example: Sparse matrix multiplication
indices = torch.tensor([[0, 1], [1, 0], [1,1]]).T
values = torch.tensor([1., 2., 3.])
size = torch.Size([2, 2])

sparse_matrix = torch.sparse_coo_tensor(indices, values,
size).coalesce()
dense_matrix = torch.tensor([[1., 2.], [3.,4.]])
```

39

```
product = torch.sparse.mm(sparse_matrix, dense_matrix)
print(f"Sparse Matrix Multiplication:\n{product}")

# Note: coalesce() is called to remove duplicate entries and
sum values when indices are repeated.
```

Personal Insight: I've found it crucial to coalesce the sparse tensor, especially after manipulating the indices or values. Failing to do so can lead to unexpected behavior.

When to Use Sparse Tensors:

- When dealing with large datasets with high sparsity (e.g., > 90% zeros).
- When memory usage is a primary concern.
- When you can leverage specialized sparse linear algebra operations.

Limitations of Sparse Tensors:

- Limited support for operations compared to dense tensors.
- Potential performance overhead when converting between sparse and dense formats.
- Requires careful consideration of the sparse format and its suitability for the specific application.

Conclusion:

Sparse tensors are a valuable tool for handling data with high sparsity, offering significant savings in memory and performance. By understanding the different sparse tensor formats and how to create and manipulate them in PyTorch, you can effectively process large datasets and build more efficient deep learning models. You've now added an important instrument to your Pytorch skillset!

Chapter 3: Neural Network Building Blocks (torch.nn) - Sculpting Your Deep Learning Masterpieces

In this chapter, we'll explore the core building blocks of neural networks within the torch.nn module. You'll learn how to create custom layers, initialize parameters effectively, choose the right activation functions, and apply regularization techniques to prevent overfitting. Think of this as becoming a skilled sculptor, understanding the properties of different materials and the techniques for shaping them into beautiful and functional forms.

Why Understanding torch.nn Matters: While pre-built layers are convenient, truly mastering torch.nn allows you to create custom architectures tailored to your specific needs. You'll move beyond being a user of existing models and become a *creator* of new and innovative solutions.

3.1 Layer Construction: Custom Layers and Modules - Beyond the Basics: Unleash Your Inner Architect

While PyTorch's torch.nn module provides a treasure trove of pre-built layers, you'll inevitably reach a point where you need to create custom layers to implement specific functionalities or architectures. This section is your guide to building custom layers and modules, transforming you from a user of existing tools into a creator of your own.

Why Custom Layers and Modules Matter: The ability to create custom layers unlocks a whole new level of flexibility and control. You can tailor your models to the specific characteristics of your data and implement novel architectures that go beyond the standard building blocks. It's the difference between using pre-fabricated components and designing a structure from the ground up.

Understanding the nn.Module Class: The Foundation of Custom Layers

The nn.Module class is the bedrock upon which all neural network modules in PyTorch are built. To create a custom layer or module, you *must* inherit from nn.Module. This class provides the essential functionality for managing the module's parameters, defining the forward pass, and tracking the module's state.

Key Methods:

- **__init__(self, ...):** This is the constructor of your module. Here, you define the layers and parameters that your module will use. You *must* call super().__init__() to initialize the nn.Module base class.
- **forward(self, x):** This method defines the forward pass of your module. It specifies how the input data x is processed and transformed to produce the output.

Creating a Simple Custom Linear Layer: A Step-by-Step Example

Let's start with a simple example: creating a custom linear layer that performs a linear transformation on the input data. This is essentially what nn.Linear does, but we'll build it from scratch to understand the underlying mechanics.

```python
import torch
import torch.nn as nn

class CustomLinearLayer(nn.Module):
    def __init__(self, input_size, output_size):
        super(CustomLinearLayer, self).__init__()

        # 1. Define the weight and bias as learnable
parameters
        self.weight = nn.Parameter(torch.randn(output_size,
input_size)) # output_size x input_size
        self.bias = nn.Parameter(torch.randn(output_size)) #
output_size

    def forward(self, x):
        # 2. Perform the linear transformation: y = x @ W.T +
b
        return torch.matmul(x, self.weight.T) + self.bias

# Instantiate the custom layer
input_size = 10
output_size = 5
custom_linear = CustomLinearLayer(input_size, output_size)

# Create some random input data (batch size of 1)
input_data = torch.randn(1, input_size)

# Pass the input through the custom layer
```

```
output_data = custom_linear(input_data)

print(f"Output Data Shape: {output_data.shape}") # Expected:
torch.Size([1, 5])

# Access weights and biases
print(f"Custom Linear Layer
Weights:\n{custom_linear.weight}")
print(f"Custom Linear Layer Biases:\n{custom_linear.bias}")
```

Let's break down the code:

1. **nn.Parameter:** The most critical step! Wrapping your weight and bias tensors with nn.Parameter tells PyTorch that these tensors are *learnable parameters*. Autograd will track their gradients during backpropagation, and they will be updated by the optimizer. If you forget this, your parameters won't be trained!
2. **forward Method:** The forward method defines the core logic of the layer. In this case, we perform a matrix multiplication of the input x with the transpose of the weight matrix (self.weight.T) and add the bias.

Personal Insight: I made the mistake of forgetting nn.Parameter once and spent hours debugging why my model wasn't learning! It's a subtle but crucial detail.

Building More Complex Modules: Composing Layers Together

You can create more complex modules by combining multiple layers and modules within the forward method. This allows you to build sophisticated neural network architectures.

```
    import torch
import torch.nn as nn

class CustomMLP(nn.Module):
    def __init__(self, input_size, hidden_size, output_size):
        super(CustomMLP, self).__init__()

        # Define the layers
        self.fc1 = nn.Linear(input_size, hidden_size)
        self.relu = nn.ReLU() #nn.functional.relu also works
        self.fc2 = nn.Linear(hidden_size, output_size)

    def forward(self, x):
```

```
        # Define the forward pass
        x = self.fc1(x) #First fully connected
        x = self.relu(x)  #Apply non linearity
        x = self.fc2(x) # Second Fully connected
        return x

# Instantiate the custom MLP module
input_size = 10
hidden_size = 5
output_size = 1
custom_mlp = CustomMLP(input_size, hidden_size, output_size)

# Create some random input data
input_data = torch.randn(1, input_size)

# Pass the input through the custom MLP
output_data = custom_mlp(input_data)

print(f"Output Data Shape: {output_data.shape}") #Expected:
torch.Size([1, 1])
```

In this example, we create a custom multi-layer perceptron (MLP) module with two linear layers and a ReLU activation function.

Using nn.Sequential:

For simple, sequential architectures, you can use nn.Sequential to simplify the code.

```
        import torch.nn as nn

# Custom sequential model
sequential_model = nn.Sequential(
    nn.Linear(10, 5),
    nn.ReLU(),
    nn.Linear(5, 1)
)

print(sequential_model)
```

nn.Sequential vs Custom Modules: nn.Sequential is great for simple, linear stacks of layers. However, for more complex architectures with branching paths or skip connections, you'll need to create a custom module.

Registering Buffers:

Besides parameters, layers can also have internal states, such as the running mean and variance in BatchNorm layers. Those are neither trainable parameters (i.e., updated by the optimizer) nor constants. They are called *buffers*. To register them, you can use self.register_buffer. Let's see an example where we keep track of running statistics:

```python
import torch
import torch.nn as nn

class StatisticsLayer(nn.Module):
    def __init__(self, feature_size):
        super().__init__()
        self.register_buffer("running_mean",
torch.zeros(feature_size))
        self.feature_size = feature_size

    def forward(self, x):
        assert x.shape[1] == self.feature_size
        mean = x.mean(dim=0)
        self.running_mean = 0.99 * self.running_mean + 0.01 *
mean
        return x

#Initialize the Layer and test it.
stat_layer = StatisticsLayer(feature_size=3)
test_data  = torch.randn(5, 3)
test_output = stat_layer(test_data)

print(stat_layer.running_mean)
```

Common Pitfalls and Best Practices:

- **Forgetting super().__init__():** This is a common mistake that can lead to unexpected behavior. *Always* call super().__init__() in your __init__ method.
- **Not Using nn.Parameter:** As mentioned earlier, remember to wrap your weight and bias tensors with nn.Parameter to tell PyTorch that they are learnable parameters.
- **Initializing Parameters Correctly:** Ensure your parameters are initialized correctly to avoid training issues.
- **Documenting Your Layers:** Add clear documentation to your custom layers to explain their functionality and inputs/outputs.

Personal Insight: I've found that writing unit tests for my custom layers is a great way to ensure that they are working correctly.

Conclusion:

You've now mastered the art of creating custom layers and modules in PyTorch! You can now build custom models tailored to your specific needs. This skill is the doorway to pushing deep learning forward and designing unique architectures. In the next section, we'll delve into parameter initialization strategies.

3.2 Parameter Initialization Strategies: Setting the Stage for Learning - Giving Your Network a Fighting Chance

The way you initialize the parameters (weights and biases) of your neural network can have a profound impact on its training dynamics and ultimate performance. Poor initialization can lead to slow convergence, vanishing gradients, exploding gradients, or even prevent your network from learning at all. Proper parameter initialization is like giving your network a solid foundation to build upon – setting it up for success from the very beginning. Think of it as tuning a musical instrument – if it's not properly tuned, the music will sound off-key.

Why Parameter Initialization Matters: A well-initialized network can converge faster, achieve better accuracy, and be more robust to different training conditions. Don't underestimate the power of this often-overlooked aspect of deep learning.

The Importance of Variance: Keeping Signals Flowing

The primary goal of parameter initialization is to ensure that the variance of the activations and gradients remains consistent across layers. This prevents the signals from either vanishing (becoming too small) or exploding (becoming too large) as they propagate through the network. If the signal dies out, the downstream layers will not be trained as effectively. If they explode, the optimization procedure becomes highly unstable.

Common Initialization Strategies: A Guided Tour

Let's explore some of the most common and effective parameter initialization strategies:

- **Constant Initialization:** This is the simplest initialization strategy, where all parameters are initialized to the same constant value (e.g.,

0, 1, 0.01). While simple, it's rarely a good choice, as it can lead to symmetry breaking issues, where all neurons in a layer learn the same thing. Biases are often initialized to zero.

- **Random Initialization (Uniform and Normal Distributions):** This involves drawing random values from a uniform or normal distribution. While better than constant initialization, it doesn't take into account the size of the layers, which can still lead to vanishing or exploding gradients.
- **Xavier/Glorot Initialization:** This strategy takes into account the number of inputs and outputs of a layer to scale the random values appropriately. It's designed to keep the variance of the activations consistent across layers and is particularly well-suited for layers with sigmoid or tanh activation functions.
- **He Initialization (Kaiming Initialization):** This is a variant of Xavier initialization that is specifically designed for layers with ReLU activation functions. It scales the random values based on the number of inputs to the layer, taking into account the ReLU's tendency to "kill" neurons with negative inputs.
- **Orthogonal Initialization:** This strategy initializes the weight matrix to be an orthogonal matrix. Orthogonal matrices have the property that their rows (and columns) are orthonormal (i.e., they are mutually perpendicular and have unit length). This can improve training stability, especially in recurrent neural networks.

```
import torch
import torch.nn as nn

# Example: Applying different initialization strategies
linear_layer = nn.Linear(10, 5) # Example layer for
initializations

# 1. Constant Initialization
with torch.no_grad():
    nn.init.constant_(linear_layer.bias, 0)  # Initialize
biases to 0
    print(f"Constant Initialization -
Bias:\n{linear_layer.bias}")

# 2. Random Uniform Initialization:
with torch.no_grad():
    nn.init.uniform_(linear_layer.weight, a=-0.1, b=0.1)
#Range -0.1 to 0.1
    print(f"Uniform Initialization -
Weight:\n{linear_layer.weight}")

# 3. Random Normal Initialization:
```

```
with torch.no_grad():
    nn.init.normal_(linear_layer.weight, mean=0.0, std=0.02)
#Mean 0, std dev 0.02
    print(f"Normal Initialization -
Weight:\n{linear_layer.weight}")



# 4. Xavier/Glorot Initialization:
with torch.no_grad():
    nn.init.xavier_uniform_(linear_layer.weight)   # Xavier
Uniform Initialization
    print(f"Xavier Uniform Initialization -
Weight:\n{linear_layer.weight}")

# 5. He/Kaiming Initialization:
with torch.no_grad():
    nn.init.kaiming_uniform_(linear_layer.weight,
nonlinearity='relu')   # He Initialization (ReLU)
    print(f"He Uniform Initialization -
Weight:\n{linear_layer.weight}")

# 6. Orthogonal Initialization
with torch.no_grad():
    nn.init.orthogonal_(linear_layer.weight)
    print(f"Orthogonal Initialization -
Weight:\n{linear_layer.weight}")
```

Important Notes:

- Remember to apply the initialization *within* a torch.no_grad()
  context. This prevents the initialization operations from being tracked
  by Autograd. We only want the network's parameters to change due
  to the optimization algorithm.
- The nonlinearity argument in nn.init.kaiming_uniform_() and
  nn.init.kaiming_normal_() specifies the activation function used in
  the layer. This is important for scaling the initialization appropriately.

Personal Insight: I've found that using the appropriate initialization strategy
can significantly speed up training, especially for deep networks. He
initialization is my go-to choice for ReLU-based networks, while Xavier
initialization is a good starting point for networks with sigmoid or tanh
activations.

Choosing the Right Strategy: A Practical Guide

The best initialization strategy depends on the specific architecture and activation functions used in your network. Here's a practical guide:

- **ReLU Activations:** Use He initialization (Kaiming initialization).
- **Sigmoid or Tanh Activations:** Use Xavier/Glorot initialization.
- **Recurrent Neural Networks (RNNs):** Consider orthogonal initialization to improve training stability.
- **Custom Architectures:** Experiment with different initialization strategies to find what works best.

When to Deviate from the Norm:

While these are good guidelines, there are situations where you might want to deviate from the standard recommendations. For example, if you're using a very deep network with residual connections, you might need to experiment with different initialization scales to prevent vanishing gradients.

Advanced Techniques: Spectral Normalization:

Another advanced technique for stabilizing training is spectral normalization. This technique normalizes the spectral norm (the largest singular value) of the weight matrices, preventing them from becoming too large and causing exploding gradients.

Conclusion

Proper parameter initialization is a crucial step in setting your neural network up for success. By understanding the different initialization strategies and their underlying principles, you can significantly improve your network's training dynamics and performance. It is the secret weapon to unlocking its true potential! In the next section, we'll explore activation functions and their role in introducing non-linearity into your models.

3.3 Activation Functions: Choosing the Right Activation - Introducing Non-Linearity: Giving Your Network the Power to Learn

Activation functions are the unsung heroes of neural networks. They introduce non-linearity into your models, allowing them to learn complex patterns and relationships in the data. Without activation functions, a neural network would simply be a linear regression model, severely limiting its ability to represent real-world phenomena. Think of activation functions as the secret sauce that gives your network the power to learn and generalize. They add the unique flavoring that elevates a dish from bland to delicious.

Why Activation Functions Matter: Linear transformations alone are insufficient to model complex, non-linear relationships. Activation functions enable neural networks to approximate any continuous function, making them powerful tools for a wide range of applications.

The Role of Non-Linearity: From Linear to Complex

Neural networks without activation functions are simply linear models, which means they can only learn linear relationships between the input and output. Linear relationships are often too simplistic to capture the complexities of real-world data.

Activation functions introduce non-linearity by applying a non-linear transformation to the output of each layer. This allows the network to learn complex patterns and approximate any continuous function, in theory.

Common Activation Functions: A Detailed Exploration

Let's explore some of the most common activation functions and their characteristics:

- **Sigmoid:**
    - **Formula:** $\sigma(x) = 1 / (1 + \exp(-x))$
    - **Output Range:** (0, 1)
    - **Pros:** Squashes the input to a range between 0 and 1, making it suitable for binary classification problems.
    - **Cons:** Suffers from vanishing gradients, especially when the input is very large or very small. Not zero-centered, which can slow down training.
- **Tanh (Hyperbolic Tangent):**
    - **Formula:** $\tanh(x) = (\exp(x) - \exp(-x)) / (\exp(x) + \exp(-x))$
    - **Output Range:** (-1, 1)
    - **Pros:** Squashes the input to a range between -1 and 1, which can be helpful for centering the data.
    - **Cons:** Still suffers from vanishing gradients, although less severely than sigmoid.
- **ReLU (Rectified Linear Unit):**

- o **Formula:** ReLU(x) = max(0, x)
- o **Output Range:** $[0, \infty)$
- o **Pros:** Simple, computationally efficient, and alleviates the vanishing gradient problem for positive inputs.
- o **Cons:** Can suffer from the "dying ReLU" problem, where neurons get stuck in an inactive state and stop learning. Not zero-centered.
- **Leaky ReLU:**
  - o **Formula:** Leaky ReLU(x) = x if x > 0 else αx (where α is a small positive constant)
  - o **Output Range:** $(-\infty, \infty)$
  - o **Pros:** Addresses the dying ReLU problem by allowing a small, non-zero gradient when the input is negative.
  - o **Cons:** The choice of α can be sensitive to the specific problem.
- **ELU (Exponential Linear Unit):**
  - o **Formula:** ELU(x) = x if x > 0 else α(exp(x) - 1) (where α is a positive constant)
  - o **Output Range:** $(-\alpha, \infty)$
  - o **Pros:** Similar to Leaky ReLU, but can provide better regularization and robustness to noise.
  - o **Cons:** More computationally expensive than ReLU and Leaky ReLU.
- **Swish:**
  - o **Formula:** Swish(x) = x * sigmoid(x)
  - o **Output Range:** (-0.27, infinity)
  - o **Pros:** It was discovered by machine learning. Studies show it often performs better than ReLU
  - o **Cons:** Computationally expensive.

```
import torch
import torch.nn as nn
import torch.nn.functional as F  # Functional versions of
activation functions

# Example: Using different activation functions

input_data = torch.randn(1, 10)  # Create some random input
data

# 1. Sigmoid
sigmoid_output = torch.sigmoid(input_data)
print(f"Sigmoid Output: {sigmoid_output}")

# 2. Tanh
```

```
tanh_output = torch.tanh(input_data)
print(f"Tanh Output: {tanh_output}")

# 3. ReLU (using nn.ReLU)
relu_layer = nn.ReLU()
relu_output = relu_layer(input_data) # Object Oriented Way
print(f"ReLU Output (nn.ReLU): {relu_output}")

# 4. ReLU (using F.relu - Functional Form)
relu_output_functional = F.relu(input_data) #Functional way -
no parameters.
print(f"ReLU Output (F.relu): {relu_output_functional}")

# 5. Leaky ReLU
leaky_relu_layer = nn.LeakyReLU(negative_slope=0.01)   #
Define the negative slope
leaky_relu_output = leaky_relu_layer(input_data)
print(f"Leaky ReLU Output: {leaky_relu_output}")

# 6. ELU
elu_layer = nn.ELU(alpha=1.0)   # Define the alpha value
elu_output = elu_layer(input_data)
print(f"ELU Output: {elu_output}")

#7. Swish
swish_output = input_data * torch.sigmoid(input_data)
print(f"Swish Output: {swish_output}")
```

Personal Insight: I've found that ReLU and its variants (Leaky ReLU, ELU) are generally the best choice for hidden layers in deep neural networks. They tend to train faster and achieve better performance than sigmoid or tanh. However, sigmoid is still useful in the output layer for binary classification problems.

Choosing the Right Activation: A Practical Guide

The best activation function for your specific problem will depend on several factors, including the architecture of your network, the nature of your data, and the desired output range. Here's a general guide:

- **Hidden Layers:**
    - **ReLU:** A good starting point for many applications.
    - **Leaky ReLU or ELU:** Can help mitigate the vanishing gradient problem, especially in deep networks.
- **Output Layers:**

- ○ **Sigmoid:** For binary classification problems (output range of 0 to 1).
- ○ **Softmax:** For multi-class classification problems (output probabilities for each class).
- ○ **Linear (No Activation):** For regression problems.

When to Experiment:

Don't be afraid to experiment with different activation functions to see what works best for your specific problem. There's no one-size-fits-all solution. The more you practice, the more intuitive it will become.

Conclusion

By understanding the properties of different activation functions and their role in introducing non-linearity, you can make informed decisions about which activation functions to use in your neural networks. This understanding is pivotal as it gives you the ability to transform a standard model into a robust learning machine. In the next section, we'll explore regularization techniques for preventing overfitting and improving the generalization performance of your models.

3.4 Regularization Techniques: Dropout, BatchNorm, Weight Decay - Preventing Overfitting: Building Robust Models

One of the biggest challenges in deep learning is preventing overfitting – the phenomenon where your model learns the training data *too well*, memorizing the noise and specific details rather than learning the underlying patterns. An overfit model performs well on the training data but generalizes poorly to new, unseen data. Regularization techniques are your arsenal against overfitting, helping you build models that are more robust and generalize better. Think of them as training wheels for your network – helping it learn to balance and generalize without falling over.

Why Regularization Matters: Regularization allows you to train more complex models without sacrificing generalization performance. It's essential for building models that can perform well in real-world scenarios where the data is often noisy and imperfect.

Understanding Overfitting: Memorization vs. Generalization

Overfitting occurs when your model learns the training data so well that it essentially memorizes it. This results in a model that performs exceptionally well on the training data but poorly on new, unseen data.

Signs of Overfitting:

- Large gap between training accuracy and validation accuracy.
- Model complexity that is too high for the amount of available data.
- Sensitivity to small changes in the training data.

Common Regularization Techniques: A Detailed Exploration

Let's explore some of the most common and effective regularization techniques in PyTorch:

- **Dropout:**
    - **Concept:** Randomly deactivates a fraction of the neurons (and their connections) during each training iteration. This forces the network to learn more robust features that are not dependent on any particular neuron.
    - **Implementation:** Use the nn.Dropout layer in PyTorch. Specify the probability p of dropping out each neuron (typically between 0.2 and 0.5).
- **Batch Normalization (BatchNorm):**
    - **Concept:** Normalizes the activations of each layer within a mini-batch, improving training stability and reducing the risk of vanishing or exploding gradients. Also, it can have a regularization effect.
    - **Implementation:** Use the nn.BatchNorm1d layer for fully connected layers and nn.BatchNorm2d for convolutional layers. The normalization is applied to each feature channel independently.
- **Weight Decay (L2 Regularization):**
    - **Concept:** Adds a penalty to the loss function based on the magnitude of the weights, encouraging the model to learn smaller weights and prevent overfitting. The penalty is proportional to the sum of the squares of the weights.
    - **Implementation:** Specify the weight_decay parameter in the optimizer (e.g., torch.optim.Adam(model.parameters(), lr=0.001, weight_decay=0.01)).

```python
import torch
import torch.nn as nn

# Example: Applying regularization techniques

# 1. Dropout
dropout_layer = nn.Dropout(p=0.5)  # Dropout with a
probability of 0.5
input_data = torch.randn(1, 10)
dropout_output = dropout_layer(input_data)
print(f"Dropout Output: {dropout_output}")

# 2. Batch Normalization
batchnorm_layer = nn.BatchNorm1d(num_features=10)  # Batch
Normalization for 1D data
input_data = torch.randn(1, 10)
batchnorm_output = batchnorm_layer(input_data)
print(f"BatchNorm Output: {batchnorm_output}")

# 3. Weight Decay (L2 Regularization)
linear_layer = nn.Linear(10, 5)
optimizer = torch.optim.Adam(linear_layer.parameters(),
lr=0.001, weight_decay=0.01)  # Weight Decay (L2)
print(f"Optimizer with Weight Decay: {optimizer}")

#Example of L1 Regularization/Sparsity (less common in DL,
but useful)
def l1_regularization(model, lambda_l1=0.01):
  lossL1 = 0.0
  for param in model.parameters():
    lossL1 = lossL1 + torch.norm(param, 1) #L1 norm
  return lambda_l1 * lossL1
```

Practical Explanation:

- Dropout: The dropout layer randomly sets some of the input elements to zero during the forward pass. This prevents neurons from co-adapting too much and forces the network to learn more robust features.
- BatchNorm: Batch Normalization normalizes each feature across a batch of data, making the training process more stable and allowing for higher learning rates.
- Weight Decay: The weight decay adds a penalty to the loss function proportional to the sum of the squared weights. It encourages the network to use smaller weights, making the model simpler and less prone to overfitting.

Personal Insight: I've found that a combination of dropout, batch normalization, and weight decay is often the most effective approach for preventing overfitting. However, it's important to tune the hyperparameters (e.g., dropout probability, weight decay coefficient) to find the best configuration for your specific model and dataset.

Choosing the Right Regularization: A Practical Guide

The best regularization techniques for your specific problem will depend on several factors, including the size of your dataset, the complexity of your model, and the characteristics of your data. Here's a general guide:

- **Small Datasets:** Use stronger regularization techniques, such as high dropout probability and large weight decay coefficient.
- **Large Datasets:** Use weaker regularization techniques, or even no regularization at all.
- **Complex Models:** Use stronger regularization techniques to prevent overfitting.
- **Simple Models:** Use weaker regularization techniques, or even no regularization at all.

When to Experiment:

There's no one-size-fits-all solution when it comes to regularization. It's important to experiment with different techniques and hyperparameters to find what works best for your specific problem.

Early Stopping: Monitoring Validation Performance

Another important technique for preventing overfitting is early stopping. This involves monitoring the performance of your model on a validation set during training and stopping the training process when the validation performance starts to degrade.

Conclusion

By mastering regularization techniques, you can build more robust and generalizable deep learning models that perform well in real-world scenarios. These tools are crucial for navigating the nuances of datasets and creating models that learn beyond the training data. In the next chapter, we'll explore different neural network architectures and how to build them using the building blocks we've covered in this chapter.

Chapter 4: Optimization Algorithms and Learning Rate Schedules - Navigating the Loss Landscape

In this chapter, we'll explore the optimization algorithms that power the training of neural networks. These algorithms are responsible for finding the optimal set of parameters that minimize the loss function. We'll also delve into learning rate schedules, which control how the learning rate changes during training. Think of this chapter as learning to navigate a complex mountain range to find the lowest valley - the optimal solution for your model.

Why Understanding Optimization Matters: Choosing the right optimization algorithm and learning rate schedule can significantly impact the speed of training, the final performance of your model, and its ability to generalize to new data. These are critical components for model performance.

4.1 Gradient Descent Family: SGD, Adam, RMSprop - A Journey Through Optimization: The Engine of Learning

At the heart of every deep learning model lies an optimization algorithm – the engine that drives the learning process. The gradient descent family of algorithms forms the foundation for training neural networks. These algorithms iteratively adjust the model's parameters to minimize the loss function, guiding the model towards a state where it can accurately map inputs to desired outputs.

Why Understanding Gradient Descent Matters: A deep understanding of these algorithms allows you to diagnose training issues, fine-tune hyperparameters, and choose the right optimizer for your specific task. It's like understanding how an engine works – allowing you to troubleshoot and tune it for optimal performance.

The Essence of Gradient Descent: Following the Slope Downhill

Imagine the loss function as a complex landscape with hills and valleys. The goal of gradient descent is to find the lowest point in this landscape – the point where the loss is minimized. Gradient descent achieves this by iteratively moving in the direction of the *negative gradient* of the loss function. The gradient points in the direction of steepest *ascent*, so moving in the opposite direction takes us *downhill* towards the minimum.

Key Concepts:

- **Loss Function:** A mathematical function that measures the difference between the model's predictions and the true values. The goal of training is to minimize this function.
- **Parameters:** The weights and biases of the neural network that are adjusted during training.
- **Gradient:** A vector that points in the direction of steepest ascent of the loss function.
- **Learning Rate:** A hyperparameter that controls the step size taken in the direction of the negative gradient.

Exploring the Variants: SGD, Adam, and RMSprop

Let's delve into three of the most popular gradient descent variants:

- **Stochastic Gradient Descent (SGD): The Foundation**
  - **Concept:** SGD updates the parameters using the gradient computed on a *single* mini-batch of data (or even a single data point). This makes it computationally efficient but also introduces a lot of noise into the training process.
  - **Implementation:** In PyTorch, you can use the torch.optim.SGD class.
  - **Pros:** Simple to understand and implement. Computationally efficient for large datasets.
  - **Cons:** Can be slow to converge, especially in complex loss landscapes. Sensitive to the choice of learning rate and can easily get stuck in local minima. The noisy updates can cause oscillations.
- **Adam (Adaptive Moment Estimation): Adapting to the Terrain**
  - **Concept:** Adam combines the ideas of *momentum* and *adaptive learning rates* to improve convergence speed and stability. It maintains estimates of both the first moment (mean) and the second moment (variance) of the gradients, using these estimates to adaptively adjust the learning rate for each parameter.
  - **Implementation:** In PyTorch, you can use the torch.optim.Adam class.

- o **Pros:** Generally converges faster than SGD and is less sensitive to the choice of learning rate. Often a good first choice for many problems.
- o **Cons:** More computationally expensive than SGD. Can sometimes over-generalize.
- **RMSprop (Root Mean Square Propagation): Taming Oscillations**
  - o **Concept:** RMSprop also uses adaptive learning rates but focuses on dampening oscillations in the gradients. It maintains a running average of the squared gradients and divides the learning rate for each parameter by the square root of this average. This helps to prevent the learning rate from becoming too large in directions with frequent oscillations.
  - o **Implementation:** In PyTorch, you can use the torch.optim.RMSprop class.
  - o **Pros:** Can converge faster than SGD and is less sensitive to the choice of learning rate, especially for non-stationary objectives.
  - o **Cons:** More computationally expensive than SGD.

```
import torch
import torch.nn as nn
import torch.optim as optim

# Example: Using different optimization algorithms in PyTorch

# Create a simple linear layer (example)
linear_layer = nn.Linear(10, 5)

# 1. Stochastic Gradient Descent (SGD)
optimizer_sgd = optim.SGD(linear_layer.parameters(), lr=0.01)
#0.01 is example.
print(f"SGD Optimizer:\n{optimizer_sgd}")

# 2. Adam (Adaptive Moment Estimation)
optimizer_adam = optim.Adam(linear_layer.parameters(),
lr=0.001)   # 0.001 is example.
print(f"Adam Optimizer:\n{optimizer_adam}")

# 3. RMSprop (Root Mean Square Propagation)
optimizer_rmsprop = optim.RMSprop(linear_layer.parameters(),
lr=0.001) #0.001 is example
print(f"RMSprop Optimizer:\n{optimizer_rmsprop}")

# Example Training loop
# Sample inputs and Target outputs
inputs = torch.randn(64, 10) #Batch size of 64 with feature
size of 10
```

```
targets = torch.randn(64, 5)   #Batch size of 64 with output
size of 5.
criterion = nn.MSELoss()       #Mean Squared Error Loss

# Pick an optimizer
optimizer = optimizer_adam # or any other optimizer

# Perform training
num_epochs = 2

for epoch in range(num_epochs):
  #Zero gradient buffers
  optimizer.zero_grad()    #Reset gradients before each pass
  outputs = linear_layer(inputs) #Perform the forward pass
  loss = criterion(outputs, targets) #Calculate the loss
  loss.backward()          #Backpropogate the gradients
  optimizer.step()         #Update the weights!

  print(f"Epoch [{epoch+1}/{num_epochs}], Loss:
{loss.item():.4f}") #Report Loss
```

Personal Insight: I often compare choosing an optimizer to choosing a car for a road trip. SGD is like a basic, fuel-efficient car that can get you there but may not be the most comfortable or fastest. Adam is like a luxury SUV that offers a smooth ride and good performance but can be more expensive. RMSprop is like a reliable sedan that handles well in different conditions.

Choosing the Right Optimizer: A Practical Guide

The best optimizer for your specific problem will depend on several factors, including the complexity of the loss landscape, the size of your dataset, and the available computational resources. Here's a general guide:

- **Adam:** A good starting point for many problems. It often converges quickly and is relatively insensitive to the choice of learning rate.
- **SGD with Momentum:** Can be useful for problems where Adam over-generalizes or gets stuck in sharp local minima. Requires careful tuning of the learning rate and momentum.
- **RMSprop:** A good alternative to Adam, especially when dealing with non-stationary objectives or when you want to dampen oscillations in the gradients.

When to Experiment:

Don't be afraid to experiment with different optimizers and learning rates to see what works best for your specific problem. The more you practice, the more intuitive it will become.

Conclusion

By understanding the different gradient descent algorithms and their characteristics, you can make informed decisions about which optimizer to use in your neural networks. Armed with this knowledge, you are closer to building more efficient and performant deep learning models. In the next section, we'll explore learning rate schedules and how they can further improve the training process.

4.2 Learning Rate Tuning: Schedules and Adaptive Methods - Finding the Right Pace: Orchestrating the Learning Process

The learning rate is arguably the most critical hyperparameter in deep learning. It dictates the step size taken during each update of the model's parameters, directly influencing the speed of convergence and the final performance of your model. Choosing the right learning rate is like finding the perfect tempo for a song – too fast, and the music becomes chaotic and dissonant; too slow, and it drags on and loses its energy.

Why Learning Rate Tuning Matters: A well-tuned learning rate can significantly reduce the training time, improve the model's ability to generalize to new data, and prevent it from getting stuck in local minima. This means more efficient experimentation, better results, and models that actually perform in real-world scenarios.

The Challenge of a Fixed Learning Rate: A Balancing Act

Using a fixed learning rate throughout training can be problematic. A learning rate that's too large can cause the training to diverge or oscillate wildly, while a learning rate that's too small can lead to slow convergence or getting stuck in suboptimal solutions. Finding that "Goldilocks" learning rate – just right – can be challenging and often requires significant experimentation.

Learning Rate Schedules: Adapting Over Time - A Dynamic Approach

Learning rate schedules provide a dynamic approach by adjusting the learning rate over time during the training process. This allows the model to start with a larger learning rate for faster initial progress and then gradually reduce it to fine-tune the parameters and prevent overfitting. Think of it as shifting gears while driving – starting with a lower gear for acceleration and then shifting to higher gears for cruising.

Let's explore some of the most common learning rate schedules:

- **Step Decay:** The learning rate is reduced by a factor of γ (gamma) every few epochs. This is a simple and widely used schedule.
  - Implementation:*

```
import torch
import torch.optim as optim

# Optimizer and Learning Rate
optimizer = optim.Adam(model.parameters(), lr=0.01) # Or
whatever optimizer you're using
scheduler = optim.lr_scheduler.StepLR(optimizer,
step_size=30, gamma=0.1) # Reduce LR every 30 epochs by a
factor of 0.1
```

- **Exponential Decay:** The learning rate is reduced exponentially over time.
  - *Implementation:*

```
import torch
import torch.optim as optim

# Optimizer and Learning Rate
optimizer = optim.Adam(model.parameters(), lr=0.01) # Or
whatever optimizer you're using
scheduler = optim.lr_scheduler.ExponentialLR(optimizer,
gamma=0.9) #Reduce LR by factor of 0.9 every epoch
```

- **Cosine Annealing:** The learning rate follows a cosine function, gradually decreasing and then increasing again. This can help the model escape local minima and find better solutions.
  - *Implementation:*

```
import torch
import torch.optim as optim
```

```
# Optimizer and Learning Rate
optimizer = optim.Adam(model.parameters(), lr=0.01) # Or
whatever optimizer you're using
scheduler = optim.lr_scheduler.CosineAnnealingLR(optimizer,
T_max=50, eta_min=0) #T_max is max number of iterations. lr
decays from lr to eta_min and back.
```

- **MultiStepLR:** The learning rate is reduced at specific milestone epochs.
    - ○ *Implementation:*

```
    import torch
import torch.optim as optim

# Optimizer and Learning Rate
optimizer = optim.Adam(model.parameters(), lr=0.01) # Or
whatever optimizer you're using
scheduler = optim.lr_scheduler.MultiStepLR(optimizer,
milestones=[30, 80], gamma=0.1)  # reduce at epochs 30 and 80
```

- **ReduceLROnPlateau:** The learning rate is reduced when a metric has stopped improving. Useful when combined with early stopping.
    - ○ *Implementation:*

```
    import torch
import torch.optim as optim

# Optimizer and Learning Rate
optimizer = optim.Adam(model.parameters(), lr=0.01) # Or
whatever optimizer you're using
scheduler = optim.lr_scheduler.ReduceLROnPlateau(optimizer,
mode='min', factor=0.1, patience=10)
```

- ▪ Mode can be min or max, and depends on whether the metric you are using should increase or decrease (e.g. validation loss or validation accuracy, respectively.)
- ▪ Factor is the factor by which the learning rate will be reduced.
- ▪ Patience is the number of epochs with no improvement after which the learning rate will be reduced.

Using Learning Rate Schedulers: A Step-by-Step Guide

Here's how to use learning rate schedulers in PyTorch:

1. **Create an Optimizer:** First, create an optimizer (e.g., Adam, SGD) for your model's parameters.
2. **Create a Learning Rate Scheduler:** Create a learning rate scheduler, passing in the optimizer and any necessary parameters (e.g., step_size, gamma, T_max).
3. **Update the Learning Rate:** In your training loop, call scheduler.step() *after* the optimizer.step() for all schedulers *except* ReduceLROnPlateau.

```python
import torch
import torch.nn as nn
import torch.optim as optim

# Example: Training loop with a learning rate scheduler
model = nn.Linear(10, 5)
optimizer = optim.Adam(model.parameters(), lr=0.01) #Start
with learning rate of 0.01
scheduler = optim.lr_scheduler.StepLR(optimizer,
step_size=30, gamma=0.1)  # Step decay

# Training loop
num_epochs = 50
criterion = nn.MSELoss()

for epoch in range(num_epochs):
    #Forward and loss calculations here

    # Perform the optimization step
    optimizer.zero_grad()
    outputs = model(inputs)
    loss = criterion(outputs, targets)
    loss.backward()
    optimizer.step()

    #Update the learning rate
    scheduler.step() # call after optimizer.step()

    print(f"Epoch [{epoch+1}/{num_epochs}], Loss:
{loss.item():.4f}, LR: {scheduler.get_last_lr()[0]:.6f}")
```

Personal Insight: Don't forget to call scheduler.step() in your training loop! It's a common mistake to create a scheduler but forget to actually use it. The line, scheduler.get_last_lr()[0] is very useful for monitoring and debugging.

Adaptive Learning Rate Methods: A Built-In Advantage

Adam and RMSprop are examples of adaptive learning rate methods. These algorithms automatically adjust the learning rate for each parameter based on the gradients. This eliminates the need to manually tune a global learning rate schedule, making them more convenient and often more effective.

Choosing the Right Schedule: A Practical Guide

The best learning rate schedule for your specific problem will depend on several factors, including the complexity of the loss landscape, the size of your dataset, and the available computational resources. Here's a general guide:

- **Adam or RMSprop:** Often work well with their default learning rates and don't require extensive tuning.
- **Step Decay or Exponential Decay:** Can be useful when you want to manually control the learning rate decay.
- **Cosine Annealing:** Can help the model escape local minima and find better solutions, especially in complex loss landscapes.
- **ReduceLROnPlateau:** An excellent choice when combined with early stopping.

Conclusion

Learning rate tuning is a crucial aspect of training neural networks. By understanding the different learning rate schedules and adaptive methods available in PyTorch, you can effectively control the training process and achieve optimal performance. Like a skilled conductor leading an orchestra, you can harmonize the learning rates of your model to produce beautiful and impactful results! The next topic is Momentum and its impact.

4.3 Momentum and its Impact: Accelerating Convergence - Giving Your Optimizer a Push

Imagine pushing a heavy box across a rough floor. It takes a lot of initial effort to get it moving, and it tends to stop easily due to friction. Now, imagine giving the box a strong push – it will gain momentum and continue moving more easily, even over bumps and obstacles. This analogy captures the essence of momentum in optimization.

Momentum is a technique that helps to accelerate the convergence of gradient descent algorithms by accumulating the gradients over time. It's like giving your optimizer a "push" in the right direction, helping it overcome obstacles and reach the optimal solution more quickly.

Why Momentum Matters: Momentum can significantly speed up training, improve the stability of the training process, and help the model escape local minima. It's a powerful tool for optimizing deep learning models, especially in complex loss landscapes.

The Mechanics of Momentum: Accumulating Velocity

At its core, momentum involves calculating a "velocity" vector that accumulates the past gradients. This velocity vector is then used to update the model's parameters, effectively averaging out the gradients over time.

Key Concepts:

- **Velocity (v):** A running average of the gradients, accumulating information from past updates.
- **Momentum Coefficient (β):** A hyperparameter that controls the amount of momentum applied (typically between 0.9 and 0.99). A higher value gives more weight to past gradients.
- **Learning Rate (η):** A hyperparameter that controls the step size taken in the direction of the accumulated velocity.

The Update Rule:

The update rule for SGD with momentum can be expressed as follows:

1. Calculate the gradient of the loss function with respect to the parameters (g).
2. Update the velocity vector: $v = \beta v + g$ (where β is the momentum coefficient).
3. Update the parameters: $\theta = \theta - \eta v$ (where η is the learning rate).

Diving into the Code: Implementing Momentum in PyTorch

Implementing momentum in PyTorch is straightforward. You simply specify the momentum parameter when creating your optimizer.

```
import torch
```

```python
import torch.nn as nn
import torch.optim as optim

# Example: Using SGD with momentum

# Create a linear layer (example)
linear_layer = nn.Linear(10, 5)

# Create an SGD optimizer with momentum
optimizer_sgd_momentum = optim.SGD(linear_layer.parameters(),
lr=0.01, momentum=0.9)

print(f"SGD Optimizer with
Momentum:\n{optimizer_sgd_momentum}")

# Example Training loop
# Sample inputs and Target outputs
inputs = torch.randn(64, 10) #Batch size of 64 with feature
size of 10
targets = torch.randn(64, 5)  #Batch size of 64 with output
size of 5.
criterion = nn.MSELoss()      #Mean Squared Error Loss

# Perform training
num_epochs = 2

for epoch in range(num_epochs):
  #Zero gradient buffers
  optimizer_sgd_momentum.zero_grad()    #Reset gradients
before each pass
  outputs = linear_layer(inputs) #Perform the forward pass
  loss = criterion(outputs, targets) #Calculate the loss
  loss.backward()            #Backpropogate the gradients
  optimizer_sgd_momentum.step()         #Update the weights!

  print(f"Epoch [{epoch+1}/{num_epochs}], Loss:
{loss.item():.4f}") #Report Loss
```

Practical Explanation:

- The momentum parameter in torch.optim.SGD specifies the momentum coefficient (β). A value of 0.9 is a common choice.

The Benefits of Momentum: Smoothing and Acceleration

Momentum offers several key benefits:

- **Accelerated Convergence:** By accumulating the gradients over time, momentum helps the optimizer to move more quickly towards the minimum, especially in directions with consistent gradients.
- **Dampened Oscillations:** Momentum smooths out the oscillations that can occur in SGD, especially when the learning rate is relatively high.
- **Escape from Local Minima:** Momentum can help the optimizer to escape from shallow local minima, allowing it to find better solutions.

Personal Insight: I often visualize momentum as a ball rolling down a hill. The momentum of the ball helps it to overcome small bumps and obstacles, allowing it to reach the bottom of the hill more quickly.

Tuning the Momentum Coefficient: Striking the Right Balance

The momentum coefficient (β) controls the amount of momentum applied. A higher value gives more weight to past gradients, while a lower value gives more weight to the current gradient.

- **High Momentum (e.g., 0.99):** Can lead to faster convergence but also increases the risk of overshooting the minimum.
- **Low Momentum (e.g., 0.5):** Provides less acceleration but can be more stable.
- **Common Value (e.g., 0.9):** A good starting point for many problems.

The optimal value of the momentum coefficient will depend on the specific problem and the characteristics of the loss landscape.

Nesterov Momentum: A Refinement

Nesterov momentum is a variant of momentum that can often lead to faster convergence. It involves evaluating the gradient at a "lookahead" position, taking into account the momentum term. In PyTorch, you can enable Nesterov momentum by setting the nesterov parameter to True in torch.optim.SGD.

Momentum in Adaptive Optimizers: Adam and RMSprop

While we've focused on SGD with momentum, the concepts of momentum are also incorporated into adaptive optimizers like Adam and RMSprop.

Adam, in particular, maintains estimates of both the first moment (mean) and the second moment (variance) of the gradients, effectively combining momentum with adaptive learning rates.

Conclusion

Momentum is a powerful technique for accelerating the convergence of gradient descent algorithms. By accumulating the gradients over time, momentum helps the optimizer to overcome obstacles and reach the optimal solution more quickly. These accumulated gradients enable your model to adapt and learn from experience, ultimately creating more robust results! Momentum is a critical piece for you Pytorch journey! Next up: Advanced Optimization.

4.4 Advanced Optimization Methods (LBFGS, etc.): Beyond the Basics - Exploring the Optimization Frontier

While Stochastic Gradient Descent (SGD) and its adaptive variants like Adam and RMSprop are the workhorses of deep learning, there exists a class of advanced optimization methods that can be valuable in certain situations. These methods often leverage information about the curvature of the loss landscape to accelerate convergence and find better solutions. Think of them as specialized tools in your optimization toolbox, reserved for specific situations where they can provide a significant advantage.

Why Explore Advanced Optimization Methods? While not always the best choice for large-scale deep learning, understanding these methods can broaden your optimization toolkit and provide alternative approaches for specific problems.

LBFGS (Limited-Memory Broyden-Fletcher-Goldfarb-Shanno): Approximating the Curvature

LBFGS is a quasi-Newton method that approximates the Hessian matrix (the matrix of second derivatives) to accelerate convergence. Newton's method uses the Hessian to directly compute the optimal step size and direction. However, computing and inverting the Hessian can be computationally expensive, especially for large models. LBFGS addresses this by approximating the Hessian using a limited amount of memory.

Key Concepts:

- **Hessian Matrix:** The matrix of second derivatives of the loss function. It provides information about the curvature of the loss landscape.
- **Quasi-Newton Method:** An optimization method that approximates the Hessian matrix to avoid the computational cost of computing it directly.
- **Limited-Memory:** LBFGS uses a limited amount of memory to store the history of gradients and updates, allowing it to scale to larger problems than traditional Newton's methods.

When to Consider LBFGS:

- **Small Datasets:** LBFGS often requires full-batch training, which means it's only suitable for datasets that can fit into memory.
- **Smooth Loss Landscapes:** LBFGS works best when the loss landscape is relatively smooth and well-behaved.
- **Few Parameters:** Problems with only a few parameters.

Implementation in PyTorch:

```
import torch
import torch.nn as nn
import torch.optim as optim

# Create a linear layer (example)
linear_layer = nn.Linear(10, 5)

# Create an LBFGS optimizer
optimizer_lbfgs = optim.LBFGS(linear_layer.parameters(),
lr=0.01) #Can be more memory intensive

print(f"LBFGS Optimizer:\n{optimizer_lbfgs}")
```

Limitations of LBFGS:

- **Memory Intensive:** Although it's a "limited-memory" method, LBFGS can still require significant memory, especially for large models.
- **Full-Batch Training:** LBFGS typically requires full-batch training, which can be impractical for large datasets.
- **Not Well-Suited for Noisy Objectives:** LBFGS can struggle with noisy loss landscapes, where the gradients are highly variable.

- **Requires Closure Function:** The LBFGS optimizer requires a closure function that reevaluates the model and returns the loss.

Example with Closure:

```python
import torch
import torch.nn as nn
import torch.optim as optim

# Create a linear layer (example)
linear_layer = nn.Linear(10, 5)
criterion = nn.MSELoss()
inputs = torch.randn(100, 10) #Full batch size of 100
targets = torch.randn(100, 5)

# Create an LBFGS optimizer
optimizer_lbfgs = optim.LBFGS(linear_layer.parameters(),
lr=0.01) #Can be more memory intensive

# Define the closure function
def closure():
  optimizer_lbfgs.zero_grad()
  outputs = linear_layer(inputs)
  loss = criterion(outputs, targets)
  loss.backward()
  return loss

# Perform optimization step (needs to be called repeatedly)
loss = optimizer_lbfgs.step(closure)

print(f"LBFGS Loss: {loss.item()}")
```

Personal Insight: I've rarely used LBFGS in my deep learning projects due to its memory requirements and full-batch training requirement. However, it can be a good choice for small-scale optimization tasks or when you need to achieve very high accuracy.

Other Advanced Optimization Methods:

Besides LBFGS, there are other advanced optimization methods that you might encounter:

- **Adahessian:** An optimizer that uses an approximation of the Hessian diagonal to scale the learning rate for each parameter, similar to Adam but with second-order information. Can be useful for training certain types of models, but can also be memory-intensive.

- **Newton-CG:** A truncated Newton method that uses conjugate gradient to solve the Newton update step. It can be more efficient than LBFGS for very large problems but requires careful tuning.

Conclusion

While not always the first choice for large-scale deep learning, advanced optimization methods like LBFGS can be valuable tools in your optimization arsenal. These techniques can offer faster convergence and better solutions for specific problems, but it's important to understand their limitations and use them judiciously. This addition to your toolkit will allow you to evaluate various approaches for different challenges and allow you to be ready for every scenario. The following chapter will delve into data handling and preprocessing.

Chapter 5: Data Handling and Preprocessing - Preparing Your Data for Deep Learning Success

In the realm of deep learning, the quality and preparation of your data are just as crucial as the architecture of your model and the choice of optimization algorithm. As the saying goes: "Garbage in, garbage out!" Proper data handling and preprocessing are essential for training models that are accurate, robust, and generalizable. Think of this chapter as learning to be a master chef, carefully selecting and preparing your ingredients to create a delicious and satisfying meal.

Why Data Handling and Preprocessing Matter: These techniques allow you to feed your model data in a format that it can understand and learn from effectively, leading to faster convergence, improved performance, and better generalization.

5.1 Custom Datasets and DataLoaders: Efficient Data Pipelines - Taking Control of Your Data Flow: Building the Foundation for Effective Training

At the heart of any deep learning project lies data. The way you structure, load, and manage your data is critical to the success of your model. PyTorch's torch.utils.data module offers the flexibility to create custom datasets and data loaders, empowering you to build efficient data pipelines tailored to your specific needs. Think of it as building a sophisticated conveyor belt system that efficiently feeds your model with the right data at the right time.

Why Custom Datasets and DataLoaders Matter: These tools enable you to:

- Handle data from diverse sources (files, databases, APIs).
- Apply custom preprocessing and transformations.
- Load data in batches for efficient training.
- Parallelize data loading to speed up the training process.

Understanding the Dataset Class: The Blueprint for Your Data

The Dataset class is an abstract class that represents a collection of data samples. To create a custom dataset, you must subclass the Dataset class and implement three essential methods:

- **__init__(self, ...):** This is the constructor of your dataset. Here, you load the data, perform any necessary preprocessing, and initialize any relevant variables.
- **__len__(self):** This method returns the total number of samples in the dataset.
- **__getitem__(self, idx):** This method retrieves a single sample (input and label) from the dataset based on the given index idx.

Let's illustrate this with a concrete example using synthetic data:

```python
import torch
from torch.utils.data import Dataset, DataLoader

# 1. Define a Custom Dataset
class MyCustomDataset(Dataset):
    def __init__(self, data, labels):
        # Load data and labels from your source (e.g., files,
databases)
        self.data = torch.tensor(data, dtype=torch.float32)
#Convert data to tensors
        self.labels = torch.tensor(labels,
dtype=torch.float32) #Convert labels to tensors

    def __len__(self):
        # Return the total number of samples
        return len(self.data)

    def __getitem__(self, idx):
        # Retrieve a sample based on its index
        return self.data[idx], self.labels[idx]

# 2. Sample data (In real use case, this would be loading
files)
data = [[1, 2, 3, 4], [5, 6, 7, 8], [9, 10, 11, 12]]
labels = [0, 1, 0]

# 3. Instantiate the Dataset
dataset = MyCustomDataset(data, labels)
```

Digging Deeper into __getitem__:

The __getitem__ method is the heart of your custom dataset. It defines how each data sample is retrieved and prepared for training. This method typically involves:

1. Loading the data from your source (e.g., reading an image from a file).
2. Performing any necessary preprocessing or transformations (e.g., resizing, normalizing, data augmentation).
3. Returning the processed data and its corresponding label.

Personal Insight: I often use custom datasets to load data from different file formats, such as CSV files, image directories, or even custom data structures. The __getitem__ method allows me to handle these diverse data sources in a uniform and efficient manner.

The DataLoader Class: Batching and Shuffling for Efficient Training

The DataLoader class provides a convenient way to iterate over your dataset in batches, shuffle the data, and load it in parallel using multiple worker processes. This significantly speeds up the training process, especially for large datasets.

Key DataLoader Parameters:

- **dataset:** The Dataset object to load data from.
- **batch_size:** The number of samples to load in each batch.
- **shuffle:** Whether to shuffle the data at the beginning of each epoch (typically set to True for training and False for validation/testing).
- **num_workers:** The number of subprocesses to use for data loading (can improve performance, especially for large datasets). A good practice is to set to the number of cores on your computer.
- **pin_memory:** If True, the data loader will copy tensors into CUDA pinned memory before returning them. This can improve performance when training on GPUs.
- **drop_last:** If True, and the size of the dataset is not divisible by the batch size, then the last batch is dropped.

Using the DataLoader:

```
import torch
from torch.utils.data import Dataset, DataLoader
```

```
#Assuming we have instantiated the dataset from before.
# 4. Instantiate the DataLoader
dataloader = DataLoader(dataset, batch_size=2, shuffle=True,
num_workers=2, pin_memory=True, drop_last = True) #Batch Size
of 2.

# 5. Iterate through the DataLoader
for batch_idx, (inputs, targets) in enumerate(dataloader):
    print(f"Batch {batch_idx+1}:")
    print(f"Inputs: {inputs}")
    print(f"Targets: {targets}")
```

Practical Explanation:

- The DataLoader iterates over the dataset in batches, providing you with mini-batches of data and labels that you can feed into your model.
- The shuffle=True argument ensures that the data is shuffled at the beginning of each epoch, which helps to prevent overfitting and improve generalization.
- The num_workers argument specifies the number of subprocesses to use for data loading. This can significantly speed up data loading, especially for large datasets.

Customizing Data Transformations: Adapting Data for Your Model

Often, you'll need to apply custom transformations to your data before feeding it into your model. This might involve resizing images, normalizing pixel values, or converting text to numerical representations. You can implement these transformations directly within the __getitem__ method of your custom dataset or use PyTorch's transforms module for more complex pipelines.

Personal Insight: I often use the transforms module to create complex data augmentation pipelines, applying a series of random transformations to the data during training. This helps to improve the robustness and generalizability of my models.

Conclusion

Mastering custom datasets and data loaders is essential for building efficient and scalable deep learning pipelines. By understanding the Dataset and DataLoader classes and their various options, you can effectively manage and access your data during training, enabling you to build more accurate and robust models. In the next section, we'll dive into the world of data augmentation strategies.

5.2 Data Augmentation Strategies: Expanding Your Data Horizon - Creating More From Less

In the world of deep learning, data is king. The more data you have, the better your models can learn and generalize. However, acquiring large, labeled datasets can be expensive and time-consuming. That's where data augmentation comes to the rescue!

Data augmentation involves creating new training samples by applying various transformations to the existing data. This effectively expands your dataset, improves the model's robustness to variations in the input, and helps to prevent overfitting. Think of it as cleverly manipulating your existing ingredients to create a wider variety of dishes, enhancing your culinary repertoire.

Why Data Augmentation Matters: Data augmentation allows you to:

- Train more robust models that are less sensitive to variations in the input data.
- Prevent overfitting, especially when you have limited data.
- Improve the generalization performance of your models.
- Effectively increase the size of your dataset without acquiring new data.

The Philosophy of Augmentation: Mimicking Real-World Variability

The key to effective data augmentation is to apply transformations that are representative of the real-world variations that your model will encounter. For example, if you're training a model to recognize cats in images, you might apply transformations that simulate different lighting conditions, camera angles, and poses.

Common Augmentation Techniques: A Toolbox of Transformations

Let's explore some of the most common and effective data augmentation techniques:

- **Image Data:**
  - **Geometric Transformations:** These transformations alter the spatial arrangement of pixels in the image.
    - *Random Rotations:* Rotate the image by a random angle.
    - *Random Flips:* Flip the image horizontally or vertically.
    - *Random Zooms:* Zoom in or out on the image.
    - *Random Translations:* Shift the image horizontally or vertically.
    - *Random Resized Crops:* Crop a random portion of the image and resize it to a fixed size.
  - **Color Jittering:** These transformations alter the color properties of the image.
    - *Brightness:* Adjust the overall brightness of the image.
    - *Contrast:* Adjust the contrast between the light and dark areas of the image.
    - *Saturation:* Adjust the intensity of the colors in the image.
    - *Hue:* Adjust the color tones in the image.
  - **Adding Noise and Blur:** These transformations introduce random noise or blur into the image.
    - *Gaussian Noise:* Add random Gaussian noise to the pixel values.
    - *Blurring:* Apply a blurring filter to smooth out the image.
- **Text Data:**
  - **Synonym Replacement:** Replace words with their synonyms.
  - **Back-Translation:** Translate the text to another language and then back to the original language. This can introduce subtle variations in the text.
  - **Random Insertion or Deletion:** Randomly insert or delete words in the text.
- **Audio Data:**
  - **Time Stretching:** Speed up or slow down the audio.
  - **Pitch Shifting:** Change the pitch of the audio.
  - **Adding Noise:** Add background noise to the audio.

Implementing Data Augmentation with torchvision.transforms: A Hands-On Approach

PyTorch's torchvision.transforms module provides a convenient way to implement data augmentation for image data. Let's see how it works in practice:

```python
import torch
from torchvision import transforms
from PIL import Image
import os

# 1. Define an Augmentation Pipeline: Specify each
transformation in sequence.
transform = transforms.Compose([
    transforms.RandomRotation(degrees=15),          # Rotate
randomly by 15 degrees
    transforms.RandomHorizontalFlip(),              # Flip
horizontally with a probability of 0.5
    transforms.RandomResizedCrop(224),              # Crop
random section and resize.
    transforms.ToTensor(),                          #
Convert to tensor. Important, do this LAST.
    transforms.Normalize((0.485, 0.456, 0.406), (0.229,
0.224, 0.225)) #Normalize images
])

# Create a custom Dataset for images with Transforms built in
class ImageDataset(Dataset):
  def __init__(self, image_dir, transform=None):
    self.image_dir = image_dir
    self.transform = transform
    self.image_paths = [os.path.join(image_dir, filename) for
filename in os.listdir(image_dir)] #Lists files
    self.classes = ['cat', 'dog']
  def __len__(self):
    return len(self.image_paths)

  def __getitem__(self, idx):
    image_path = self.image_paths[idx]
    image = Image.open(image_path).convert('RGB') #Some
images are in RGBA format.
    if self.transform:
      image = self.transform(image) #Transform here

    #This part is just to have sample labels. normally you
would load the labels from file.
    label = 0 if 'cat' in image_path else 1 #0 if cat, 1 if
dog
    label = torch.tensor(label, dtype=torch.long)
#CrossEntropy requires Long

    return image, label #Image with transformation
```

```
#Instantiate dataset
image_folder = "images" #Make sure this directory exist in
the same folder and contains sample images. It needs to be
structured with Cats and Dogs!
if not os.path.exists(image_folder):
  os.makedirs(image_folder)
  #Make sample cat image
  if not os.path.exists(f"{image_folder}/cat.jpg"): #Adds the
sample cat image
    with open(f"{image_folder}/cat.jpg", "w") as f:
      f.write("sample cat")
  #Make sample dog image
  if not os.path.exists(f"{image_folder}/dog.jpg"): #Adds the
sample dog image
    with open(f"{image_folder}/dog.jpg", "w") as f:
      f.write("sample dog")

dataset = ImageDataset(image_folder, transform=transform)
#Transforms are used for training, but not for testing.
```

Key Observations:

- transforms.Compose: This class allows you to chain together multiple transformations into a single pipeline.
- The order of transformations is important. You should typically convert the image to a tensor and normalize it *after* applying any geometric or color transformations.
- It is important to perform the transforms on your training data, but NOT on your testing and validation data.

Personal Insight: I've found that data augmentation is often the easiest way to improve the performance of your model, especially when you have limited data. Don't be afraid to experiment with different augmentation techniques and intensities.

Beyond torchvision.transforms: External Libraries

For more advanced data augmentation techniques, you can explore external libraries like:

- **Albumentations:** A fast and flexible image augmentation library that supports a wide range of transformations.

These libraries often provide more sophisticated transformations and can be more efficient than implementing custom transformations from scratch.

Choosing the Right Augmentation Techniques: A Practical Guide

The best augmentation techniques for your specific problem will depend on the type of data you're working with, the architecture of your model, and the real-world variations that your model will encounter. Here are some general guidelines:

- **Image Data:** Use geometric transformations to simulate different camera angles and poses. Use color jittering to simulate different lighting conditions. Add noise and blur to simulate sensor imperfections.
- **Text Data:** Use synonym replacement to introduce variations in the wording. Use back-translation to generate more diverse and natural-sounding sentences.
- **Audio Data:** Use time stretching and pitch shifting to simulate different speaking speeds and tones. Add noise to simulate background noise.

Conclusion

Data augmentation is a powerful tool for expanding your data horizon and building more robust and generalizable deep learning models. This tool provides robust methods to train from very small datasets. With the right transformation you are in the best place to extract the most from your training. In the following sections we will dive into imbalanced datasets and how to handle them.

5.3 Handling Imbalanced Datasets: Addressing Class Disparities - Leveling the Playing Field

In many real-world classification problems, the classes are not represented equally in the dataset. This is known as *class imbalance*. For instance, in medical diagnosis, the number of patients with a rare disease is often much smaller than the number of healthy individuals. Similarly, in fraud detection, the number of fraudulent transactions is typically much smaller than the number of legitimate transactions.

Why Imbalanced Datasets Matter: Imbalanced datasets can lead to biased models that perform poorly on the minority class, even if they achieve high overall accuracy. A model trained on an imbalanced dataset may simply learn to predict the majority class, ignoring the minority class altogether. This can have serious consequences in applications where the minority class is of particular interest. Think of it as a judge who favors one side of the courtroom, even if the other side has a legitimate claim.

The Impact of Class Imbalance: Skewed Performance Metrics

The primary impact of class imbalance is on the model's performance metrics. Common metrics like accuracy can be misleading, as they don't reflect the model's ability to correctly classify the minority class.

More Relevant Metrics:

- **Precision:** The fraction of positive predictions that are actually correct. High precision means fewer false positives.
- **Recall:** The fraction of actual positive cases that are correctly predicted. High recall means fewer false negatives.
- **F1-Score:** The harmonic mean of precision and recall. It provides a balanced measure of performance.
- **AUC-ROC:** Area Under the Receiver Operating Characteristic curve. It measures the model's ability to distinguish between the positive and negative classes across different classification thresholds.

Techniques for Handling Imbalanced Datasets: A Suite of Strategies

Let's explore some of the most common and effective techniques for handling imbalanced datasets:

- **Resampling:** Adjusting the number of samples in each class.
  - *Oversampling:* Increasing the number of samples in the minority class.
    - *Random Oversampling:* Duplicating existing samples in the minority class.
    - *SMOTE (Synthetic Minority Oversampling Technique):* Creating synthetic samples by interpolating between existing samples in the minority class.

- o *Undersampling:* Decreasing the number of samples in the majority class.
  - *Random Undersampling:* Randomly removing samples from the majority class.
  - *Tomek Links:* Removing pairs of instances that are close to each other but belong to different classes.
- **Class Weighting:** Assigning different weights to the classes during training.
  - o Increase weight of minority classes.
  - o Decrease weight of majority classes.
- **Cost-Sensitive Learning:** Modifying the cost of misclassification for each class.
  - o Assigning a higher cost to misclassifying minority instances.
- **Ensemble Methods:** Combining multiple models trained on different subsets of the data.
  - o *Balanced Bagging:* Creating multiple balanced subsets of the data and training a separate model on each subset.
- **Anomaly Detection Techniques:** For severe imbalances, the problem can be reframed as an anomaly detection problem.

Let's explore code implementations!

```
import torch
import torch.nn as nn
import torch.utils.data as data
import numpy as np

# 1. Class Weighting

# Sample labels (Highly unbalanced)
labels = [0, 0, 0, 0, 0, 0, 0, 0, 0, 1]

# Calculate class weights
class_counts = torch.tensor([[(labels.count(0)),
labels.count(1)]]) #Counts classes and converts to tensor
total = sum(class_counts) #Total number of classes
weights = total / class_counts #Inverted values are the
weights
norm_weights = weights / weights.sum() # Normalize weights to
1 so they don't explode

print(f"Class weights: {norm_weights}")

# Create Custom Image Dataset
# Sample inputs and Target outputs
```

```
inputs = torch.randn(64, 4) #Batch size of 64 with feature
size of 4
targets = torch.randint(0, 2, (64,))  #Batch size of 64 with
output size of 2.

# Loss Functions - CrossEntropy
class_weights_tensor = torch.tensor(norm_weights,
dtype=torch.float) #Requires float
loss_fn = nn.CrossEntropyLoss(weight = class_weights_tensor)
#Apply weighting to the loss



# 2. Oversampling with RandomOversampler (More advanced,
using library)
# This is here for demonstration. for smaller datasets, it's
more direct.
from imblearn.over_sampling import RandomOverSampler

#Sample Imbalanced data (converting to Numpy since imblearn
requires it)
features = np.array([[1, 2], [3, 4], [5, 6], [7, 8], [9,
10]]) #NumPy
labels = np.array([0, 0, 1, 0, 1]) #NumPy

#Apply OverSampling
oversampler = RandomOverSampler(sampling_strategy='minority')
# Only Oversample minority
features_oversampled, labels_oversampled =
oversampler.fit_resample(features, labels) #Apply oversampler

#Convert back to tensor!
features_tensor = torch.tensor(features_oversampled,
dtype=torch.float)
labels_tensor = torch.tensor(labels_oversampled,
dtype=torch.long)

print(f"Oversampled features tensor:\n{features_tensor}")
print(f"Oversampled labels tensor:\n{labels_tensor}")
```

Personal Insight: For class weighting, be careful in how high to set your weights, as you may over-inflate the impact. Using SMOTE is a great way to rebalance your dataset without simply repeating information. I also like using metrics such as the F1-score and AUC-ROC.

Choosing the Right Technique: A Balancing Act

The best technique for handling imbalanced datasets will depend on the specific characteristics of your data and the goals of your project. Here are some general guidelines:

- *Class Weighting:* A good starting point for many problems. It's simple to implement and doesn't require modifying the dataset.
- *Resampling:* Can be effective when the class imbalance is severe, but be careful not to oversample the minority class too much, as this can lead to overfitting. SMOTE is preferred to random oversampling.
- *Ensemble Methods:* Can be a good choice when you have a large dataset and want to improve the robustness of your model.

Conclusion

Handling imbalanced datasets is a critical skill for any deep learning practitioner. By understanding the different techniques and their trade-offs, you can build models that are fair, accurate, and perform well on all classes, not just the majority class. By addressing the imbalanced classes, you are now more ready than ever to prepare data for the best modeling! We'll address normalization and standardization next.

5.4 Data Normalization and Standardization: Scaling for Success - Leveling the Playing Field for Your Features

Before feeding data into a neural network, it's often crucial to apply data normalization or standardization. These techniques scale your data to a consistent range, ensuring that no single feature dominates the learning process due to its magnitude. Imagine a race where some runners start miles ahead – normalization and standardization bring them to the same starting line, ensuring a fair competition.

Why Data Scaling Matters: Data normalization and standardization:

- Prevent features with larger values from dominating the learning process.
- Speed up convergence by ensuring that the gradients are well-behaved.
- Improve the stability of the training process.
- Help to prevent vanishing or exploding gradients.
- Allow your model to learn effectively even with features measured in different units.

Normalization vs. Standardization: Choosing the Right Approach

While both techniques aim to scale your data, they do so in different ways:

- **Normalization:** Scales the data to a fixed range, typically between 0 and 1 (Min-Max Scaling) or -1 and 1. This is useful when you want to constrain the values of your features to a specific interval.
- **Standardization:** Scales the data to have zero mean and unit variance. This is useful when you want to remove the mean and scale the variance of your features, making them more comparable.

Min-Max Normalization: Scaling to a Specific Range

Min-Max normalization scales the data to a range between 0 and 1 by subtracting the minimum value and dividing by the range (maximum value minus minimum value).

Formula: $x' = (x - min) / (max - min)$

```python
import torch

# Sample data
data = torch.tensor([[1, 2, 3, 4], [5, 6, 7, 8], [9, 10, 11, 12]], dtype=torch.float32)

#Find min and max for each column
data_min = data.min(axis=0).values
data_max = data.max(axis=0).values

#Calculate normalized using Min-Max scaling
data_normalized = (data - data_min) / (data_max - data_min)

print(f"Normalized Data (Min-Max):\n{data_normalized}")
```

When to Use Min-Max Normalization:

- When you want to constrain the values of your features to a specific range.
- When you don't have outliers in your data.
- When you know the minimum and maximum values of your features in advance.

Standardization: Zero Mean and Unit Variance

Standardization scales the data to have zero mean and unit variance by subtracting the mean and dividing by the standard deviation.

Formula: x' = (x - mean) / std

```
import torch

# Sample data
data = torch.tensor([[1, 2, 3, 4], [5, 6, 7, 8], [9, 10, 11,
12]], dtype=torch.float32)

#Calculate mean and std for each column
data_mean = data.mean(axis=0)
data_std = data.std(axis=0)

#Standardization
data_standardized = (data - data_mean) / data_std

print(f"Standardized Data:\n{data_standardized}")
```

When to Use Standardization:

- When you want to remove the mean and scale the variance of your features.
- When you have outliers in your data (standardization is less sensitive to outliers than normalization).
- When you don't know the minimum and maximum values of your features in advance.
- If using CNN, standardization is typically preferred.

Implementing Scaling with torchvision.transforms: Seamless Integration

For image data, the torchvision.transforms module provides the transforms.Normalize transformation for standardization. It takes the mean and standard deviation of the dataset as input and applies the standardization formula to each channel of the image.

```
import torch
from torchvision import transforms
from PIL import Image

# 1. Define the Normalization Transformation
normalize_transform = transforms.Normalize(mean=[0.485,
0.456, 0.406], # Mean and std deviation values calculated
```

```
                                          std=[0.229, 0.224,
0.225])   # from ImageNet dataset

# 2. Load Sample Image with PIL
image_path = "images/cat.jpg" #Replace with an image that
exists.
image = Image.open(image_path).convert('RGB')

# 3. Convert to tensor for the transformation!
to_tensor = transforms.ToTensor()
image_tensor = to_tensor(image)

# 4. Apply Normalization
normalized_image = normalize_transform(image_tensor)
print(f"Normalized Image:\n{normalized_image}")
```

Important Notes:

- The mean and standard deviation values used in transforms.Normalize should be calculated on your training dataset.
- You should apply the same normalization or standardization to your validation and test datasets that you apply to your training dataset. This ensures that all of your data is on the same scale.
- The data needs to be a tensor before normalization transforms are applied.

Personal Insight: I always calculate the mean and standard deviation on my training data and use those values for all subsequent datasets. This ensures consistency and prevents data leakage.

Conclusion

Data normalization and standardization are essential preprocessing steps that can significantly improve the performance and stability of your deep learning models. By understanding the different techniques and their trade-offs, you can effectively scale your data and ensure that your model learns from features that are on a level playing field. With the tools now in hand, you are ready to conquer whatever challenges come your way! The best is yet to come!

Part II: Neural Network Architectures and Training

Chapter 6: Image Classification with CNNs - Seeing the World Through Convolutional Eyes

Image classification is a fundamental task in computer vision, with applications ranging from medical imaging to autonomous driving. Convolutional Neural Networks (CNNs) have revolutionized this field, achieving remarkable accuracy in classifying images. This chapter will guide you through the world of CNNs, exploring their architectures, training techniques, and best practices for building effective image classifiers. Think of this chapter as learning to build a specialized set of eyes for your computer, capable of recognizing and categorizing the visual world.

Why Image Classification with CNNs Matters: CNNs are a powerful tool for automatically extracting meaningful features from images, enabling you to build models that can accurately classify a wide range of visual objects. These networks have proven to be one of the most effective tools in modern AI.

6.1 CNN Architectures: LeNet to EfficientNet - A Historical Journey: The Evolution of Computer Vision

The landscape of Convolutional Neural Networks (CNNs) has undergone a dramatic transformation since their inception. From the early pioneers to the sophisticated and efficient models of today, each architecture has built upon the foundations laid by its predecessors, pushing the boundaries of what's possible in computer vision. This section will take you on a journey through time, exploring the key innovations and design principles that have shaped the evolution of CNNs. Think of this as visiting a museum showcasing the masterpieces of computer vision, each representing a significant step forward in the field.

Why Understand CNN Architectures? Knowing the evolution of CNNs allows you to:

- Appreciate the design choices that have led to improved performance.
- Select the right architecture for your specific task and resources.
- Adapt and modify existing architectures to create your own custom models.
- Understand the strengths and limitations of different approaches.

LeNet-5 (1998): The Foundation

LeNet-5, developed by Yann LeCun and his team, is a groundbreaking architecture that demonstrated the power of CNNs for image recognition. While relatively simple by today's standards, it laid the foundation for many of the concepts that are still used in CNNs today.

Key Features:

- **Convolutional Layers:** Extract features from the input image using convolutional filters.
- **Subsampling (Pooling) Layers:** Reduce the spatial resolution of the feature maps, making the network more robust to variations in the input.
- **Fully Connected Layers:** Classify the extracted features into different categories.
- **Tanh Activation Functions:** Introduce non-linearity into the network.
- *Practical applications:* Handwritten Digit Recognition.
- *Main Limitations:* Lack of computational ability, which could not facilitate larger datasets or networks.

AlexNet (2012): The Spark That Reignited the Field

AlexNet, designed by Alex Krizhevsky, Geoffrey Hinton, and Ilya Sutskever, achieved a landmark victory in the ImageNet Large Scale Visual Recognition Challenge (ILSVRC) in 2012. This victory marked a turning point in the field of computer vision, demonstrating the power of deep learning for image recognition.

Key Innovations:

- **Deeper Architecture:** AlexNet was significantly deeper than LeNet-5, with more convolutional layers and fully connected layers.
- **ReLU Activation Functions:** Replaced the tanh activation functions with ReLU, which allowed for faster training and better performance.
- **Dropout Regularization:** Used dropout to prevent overfitting.
- **Training on GPUs:** Leveraged the power of GPUs to train the large network more efficiently.
- *Practical applications:* Image classification.
- *Main Limitations:* Was followed up with improved models that showed the best practice

VGGNet (2014): Depth and Simplicity

VGGNet, developed by the Visual Geometry Group at Oxford, took a different approach to improving CNN performance. Instead of introducing complex modules, VGGNet focused on increasing the depth of the network while using small convolutional filters (3x3) throughout the architecture.

Key Features:

- **Uniform Architecture:** VGGNet consisted of a uniform architecture with only 3x3 convolutional filters and max pooling layers.
- **Increased Depth:** VGGNet models were significantly deeper than AlexNet, with up to 19 layers.
- *Emphasis:* Proved that depth could be an important factor in CNN design, not just size.
- *Practical applications:* Image classification.
- *Main Limitations:* Was still a large model, and inefficient in practice compared to later ones.

GoogLeNet (2014): The Inception Module - Learning Features at Multiple Scales

GoogLeNet, also known as Inception v1, introduced a novel architectural element called the "Inception module." This module allowed the network to learn features at multiple scales by using convolutional filters of different sizes in parallel.

Key Innovations:

- **Inception Module:** Used parallel convolutional filters of different sizes (1x1, 3x3, and 5x5) to capture features at multiple scales.
- **Auxiliary Classifiers:** Added auxiliary classifiers at intermediate layers to improve training.
- *Emphasis:* Allowed for models to consider different parameters that may not be seen by standard models.
- *Practical applications:* Image classification, object detection.
- *Main Limitations:* Parameters not very efficient, hard to run at a large scale.

ResNet (2015): Overcoming the Depth Barrier with Residual Connections

ResNet, developed by Kaiming He and his team at Microsoft Research, addressed a major challenge in deep learning: training very deep networks. ResNet introduced "residual connections" (also known as skip connections), which allow the network to learn identity mappings, making it easier to train networks with hundreds or even thousands of layers.

Key Innovations:

- **Residual Connections:** Allowed the network to learn identity mappings, enabling the training of much deeper networks.
- *Emphasis:* Has become a staple in network architecture design, improving robustness of results.
- *Practical applications:* Image classification, object detection, segmentation, and more.
- *Main Limitations:* High computational and memory requirements.

EfficientNet (2019): Scaling for Efficiency

EfficientNet, developed by Google, took a systematic approach to scaling CNNs. Instead of manually adjusting the depth, width, or resolution of the network, EfficientNet used a compound scaling method to optimize all three dimensions simultaneously.

Key Innovations:

- **Compound Scaling Method:** Systematically scales the depth, width, and resolution of the network based on a single scaling coefficient.
- *Emphasis:* Provided a way to more efficiently scale image networks
- *Practical applications:* Image classification, object detection, and more.
- *Main Limitations:* Still computationally expensive, though efficient.

Putting It All Together: Loading Pre-trained Models in PyTorch

PyTorch provides a convenient way to load pre-trained CNN architectures from the torchvision.models module. Let's see how it works:

```
import torch
import torch.nn as nn
from torchvision import models

# Example: Loading pre-trained CNN architectures
```

```
# 1. ResNet-18
resnet18 = models.resnet18(pretrained=True) #pretrained uses
trained weights.
print(f"ResNet-18:\n{resnet18}")

# 2. EfficientNet-b0
efficientnet_b0 = models.efficientnet_b0(pretrained=True)
print(f"EfficientNet-b0:\n{efficientnet_b0}")

#3. VGG16
vgg16 = models.vgg16(pretrained=True)
print(f"VGG16:\n{vgg16}")
```

Personal Insight: I find it fascinating to see how CNN architectures have evolved over time. Each architecture represents a creative solution to the challenges of image recognition, and understanding their history can provide valuable insights into the design principles that make them effective.

Choosing the Right Architecture: Balancing Performance and Resources

Selecting the right CNN architecture for your specific task is a balancing act between performance and resource constraints. Here are some general guidelines:

- **Small Datasets:** Start with a smaller architecture like ResNet-18 or EfficientNet-b0.
- **Large Datasets:** Consider using a deeper architecture like ResNet-50 or EfficientNet-b4.
- **Limited Computational Resources:** Opt for a smaller and more efficient architecture like MobileNet or EfficientNet-b0.
- **High Accuracy Requirements:** Explore deeper and more complex architectures like ResNet-101 or EfficientNet-b7.

Conclusion

From the pioneering LeNet-5 to the efficient and scalable EfficientNet, the evolution of CNN architectures has been driven by a constant pursuit of improved performance, efficiency, and robustness. By understanding the key innovations and design principles of these architectures, you can make informed decisions about which models to use for your specific image classification tasks. You are now ready to explore the architectures that have come before, and use the knowledge to build the next generation of image networks. In the next section, we will dive into transfer learning.

6.2 Transfer Learning: Fine-tuning Pre-trained Models - Standing on the Shoulders of Giants: Leveraging Existing Knowledge for Faster Learning

Imagine trying to learn a new musical instrument without any prior musical experience. It would be a long and arduous process. Now, imagine that you already play the piano – learning a new instrument like the guitar would be much easier, as you could transfer your knowledge of music theory, rhythm, and coordination. This is the essence of transfer learning.

Transfer learning is a powerful technique where you leverage pre-trained models (models trained on large datasets like ImageNet) and adapt them to your specific task. Instead of training a model from scratch, you "transfer" the knowledge learned by the pre-trained model to your new task, significantly reducing the amount of training data and computational resources required. Think of it as standing on the shoulders of giants, benefiting from the accumulated knowledge and expertise of others.

Why Transfer Learning Matters: Transfer learning allows you to:

- Achieve good performance with limited data.
- Reduce training time and computational resources.
- Improve the generalization performance of your models.
- Solve problems that would be impossible to tackle from scratch.

The Power of Pre-trained Models: Learning General Features

Pre-trained models, typically trained on massive datasets like ImageNet, have learned to extract general features that are useful for a wide range of computer vision tasks. These features capture information about edges, textures, shapes, and object parts. By leveraging these pre-trained features, you can avoid having to learn them from scratch on your own dataset.

Fine-tuning vs. Feature Extraction: Choosing the Right Strategy

When applying transfer learning, you have two main strategies to choose from:

- **Feature Extraction:** Freeze the weights of the pre-trained layers and train only the classification layer. This is a good option when you have a small dataset and want to avoid overfitting the pre-trained layers. The pre-trained network works only as a feature extractor, as only the final classification part is trained.
- **Fine-tuning:** Unfreeze some or all of the pre-trained layers and train them along with the classification layer. This is a good option when you have a larger dataset and want to adapt the pre-trained features to your specific task.

Let's illustrate this with code:

```python
import torch
import torch.nn as nn
from torchvision import models

# 1. Load a Pre-trained Model
resnet18 = models.resnet18(pretrained=True)

# 2. Freeze Pre-trained Layers (Feature Extraction)
for param in resnet18.parameters():
    param.requires_grad = False #Disable gradients for pre-
trained layers.

# 3. Modify the Classification Layer: Match output dimensions
num_ftrs = resnet18.fc.in_features
resnet18.fc = nn.Linear(num_ftrs, 10) #Change the final
dimension.
#Now you have a resnet with a new final layer trained on your
custom dimension

#Fine Tuning vs Feature Extraction
#To fine tune, set param.requires_grad = True
```

Understanding requires_grad: Setting param.requires_grad = False freezes the weights of that layer, preventing them from being updated during training.

Practical Steps and Code Sample for a more complete training and validation:

```python
import torch
import torch.nn as nn
import torch.optim as optim
from torchvision import models, transforms
from torch.utils.data import DataLoader, Dataset
```

```python
from PIL import Image
import os

# Define image directory with sample images for train and
test - in directory cat and dog exist as labels.
train_directory = "images/train"
test_directory = "images/test"

#Create sample image if they don't exist
#Check to see if image directory exists
if not os.path.exists("images/train/cat"):
    #Make folder
    os.makedirs("images/train/cat")
    os.makedirs("images/train/dog")

    #Add sample dog image
    with open("images/train/dog/sample_image.jpg", "w") as f:
        f.write("sample dog")
    #Add sample cat image
    with open("images/train/cat/sample_image.jpg", "w") as f:
        f.write("sample cat")

#Check to see if image directory exists
if not os.path.exists("images/test/cat"):
    #Make folder
    os.makedirs("images/test/cat")
    os.makedirs("images/test/dog")

    #Add sample dog image
    with open("images/test/dog/sample_image.jpg", "w") as f:
        f.write("sample dog")
    #Add sample cat image
    with open("images/test/cat/sample_image.jpg", "w") as f:
        f.write("sample cat")

# Transforms for Image Processing
data_transforms = {
    'train': transforms.Compose([
        transforms.RandomResizedCrop(224),
        transforms.RandomHorizontalFlip(),
        transforms.ToTensor(),
        transforms.Normalize([0.485, 0.456, 0.406], [0.229,
0.224, 0.225])
    ]),
    'test': transforms.Compose([
        transforms.Resize(256),
        transforms.CenterCrop(224),
        transforms.ToTensor(),
        transforms.Normalize([0.485, 0.456, 0.406], [0.229,
0.224, 0.225])
    ])
```

```
}

# Data loader using ImgFolder - uses directory structure for
labels
image_datasets = {x:
models.ImageFolder(os.path.join("images", x),
data_transforms[x])
                    for x in ['train', 'test']}

#Load data, each set
dataloaders = {x:
torch.utils.data.DataLoader(image_datasets[x], batch_size=4,
                                            shuffle=True,
num_workers=4)
            for x in ['train', 'test']}

dataset_sizes = {x: len(image_datasets[x]) for x in ['train',
'test']}
class_names = image_datasets['train'].classes #Get class
names

#Check to see if GPU is available
device = torch.device("cuda:0" if torch.cuda.is_available()
else "cpu")

#Load a pre-trained model
model_ft = models.resnet18(pretrained=True)

#Freeze layers - Feature Extraction
for param in model_ft.parameters():
    param.requires_grad = False #Disable gradients for pre-
trained layers.

#Adjust layers - Match output dimensions
num_ftrs = model_ft.fc.in_features
model_ft.fc = nn.Linear(num_ftrs, 2)   #Set to 2 for cat/dog
example

#Send to CUDA
model_ft = model_ft.to(device) #Set to CUDA

#Loss function and optimizer
criterion = nn.CrossEntropyLoss()

# Observe that only parameters of final layer are being
optimized as opposed to before.
optimizer_ft = optim.Adam(model_ft.fc.parameters(), lr=0.001)

# Decay LR by a factor of 0.1 every 7 epochs - Learning rate
scheduler
```

```python
exp_lr_scheduler = optim.lr_scheduler.StepLR(optimizer_ft,
step_size=7, gamma=0.1)

def train_model(model, criterion, optimizer, scheduler,
num_epochs=2):

    #Best result
    best_acc = 0.0

    for epoch in range(num_epochs):

        # Each epoch has a training and validation phase
        for phase in ['train', 'test']:
            if phase == 'train':
                model.train()  # Set model to training mode
            else:
                model.eval()   # Set model to evaluate mode

            running_loss = 0.0
            running_corrects = 0

            # Iterate over data.
            for inputs, labels in dataloaders[phase]:

                inputs = inputs.to(device) #Send to CUDA
                labels = labels.to(device) #Send to CUDA

                # zero the parameter gradients
                optimizer.zero_grad()

                # forward
                # track history if only in train
                with torch.set_grad_enabled(phase ==
'train'):
                    outputs = model(inputs) #Get output
                    _, preds = torch.max(outputs, 1) #Predict
output
                    loss = criterion(outputs, labels)
#Calculate Loss

                    # backward + optimize only if in training
phase
                    if phase == 'train':
                        loss.backward()  #Back Propagate
                        optimizer.step() #Optimizer

                # statistics
                running_loss += loss.item() * inputs.size(0)
#Track loss
```

```
            running_corrects += torch.sum(preds ==
labels.data) #Compare preditions to labels

            if phase == 'train':
                scheduler.step() #Decay learning rate at the
END of every training phase!

            epoch_loss = running_loss / dataset_sizes[phase]
#Report results
            epoch_acc = running_corrects.double() /
dataset_sizes[phase] #Report results

            print('Epoch is complete {} Phase: {} Loss:
{:.4f} Acc: {:.4f}'.format(epoch, phase, epoch_loss,
epoch_acc))

            # deep copy the model
            if phase == 'test' and epoch_acc > best_acc:
                best_acc = epoch_acc

    print('Best test Acc: {:4f}'.format(best_acc))
    return model # Return trained model

#Run the model
trainedModel = train_model(model_ft, criterion, optimizer_ft,
exp_lr_scheduler, num_epochs=2)
```

Personal Insight: I usually start with feature extraction and then fine-tune the pre-trained layers if I have enough data. This can help to prevent overfitting and improve the generalization performance of my models. It also allows me to train the initial layer and customize it without affecting other layers.

Data Requirements:

- Feature Extraction: Smallest Datasets - the pre-trained models are only acting as a feature extraction method.
- Fine Tuning: Larger Datasets - training will occur on all layers and weights will need to be changed, this requires more data to prevent overfitting.

Choosing the Layers to Fine-tune: A Gradual Approach

When fine-tuning, you can choose to unfreeze all layers at once or gradually unfreeze layers over time. A gradual approach can be helpful for preventing overfitting and stabilizing the training process. Start by unfreezing only the classification layer and then gradually unfreeze more layers as training progresses.

Choosing the Right Learning Rate: A Delicate Balance

When fine-tuning pre-trained models, it's often a good idea to use a smaller learning rate than you would when training a model from scratch. This is because the pre-trained layers already have a good initialization, and you want to avoid making large changes to their weights.

Conclusion

Transfer learning is a powerful technique that allows you to leverage the knowledge learned by pre-trained models, achieving good performance with limited data and resources. By understanding the different strategies for transfer learning and how to implement them in PyTorch, you can significantly accelerate your deep learning projects and build models that can tackle a wide range of computer vision tasks. This gives your the tools to create robust models and explore new challenges in the field. Let's check out how we can interpret the results!

6.3 Visualizing CNNs: Understanding Feature Maps - Peeking Inside the Black Box: Unveiling What Your Network Sees

Convolutional Neural Networks (CNNs) can often feel like mysterious black boxes. They take in images and produce predictions, but what's actually happening inside? Visualizing feature maps provides a way to "peek" inside these black boxes and gain insights into how CNNs are processing information.

Feature maps represent the activations of different filters in the convolutional layers. By visualizing these feature maps, we can get a sense of what features the network is learning to detect. Think of it as analyzing the brushstrokes and color palettes of a painter to understand their artistic style.

Why Visualize Feature Maps? Visualizing feature maps allows you to:

- Understand what features the network is learning.

- Identify potential problems with your model (e.g., the network is not learning meaningful features).
- Gain intuition about how different layers contribute to the final prediction.
- Debug your model and improve its performance.

Understanding Feature Maps: The Network's Internal Representation

Each convolutional layer in a CNN learns a set of filters that detect specific patterns in the input data. When an image is passed through a convolutional layer, each filter produces a feature map that represents the strength of the filter's response at different locations in the image.

Key Concepts:

- **Convolutional Filters:** Small matrices that are convolved with the input image to extract features.
- **Feature Map:** A two-dimensional array that represents the activations of a particular filter at different locations in the image. Higher activations indicate a stronger response.
- **Channels:** Feature maps can have one or more channels, representing different aspects of the learned features.

Visualizing Feature Maps: A Step-by-Step Guide with Code

Let's see how to visualize feature maps in PyTorch with a practical example:

```python
import torch
import torch.nn as nn
from torchvision import models, transforms
from PIL import Image
import matplotlib.pyplot as plt
import numpy as np

# 1. Load a Pre-trained Model
resnet18 = models.resnet18(pretrained=True) #Pick from pre-
trained
resnet18.eval() #Set to eval, important to prevent batch norm
from changing.

# 2. Load and Preprocess an Image
image_path = "images/cat.jpg" #Replace this file with
another, one that exists
image = Image.open(image_path).convert('RGB') #Loads the
image
```

```python
#Apply transforms that it expects
preprocess = transforms.Compose([
    transforms.Resize(256),
    transforms.CenterCrop(224),
    transforms.ToTensor(),
    transforms.Normalize(mean=[0.485, 0.456, 0.406],
std=[0.229, 0.224, 0.225])
])
input_tensor = preprocess(image) #Turns image into tensor
input_batch = input_tensor.unsqueeze(0) # create a mini-batch
as expected by the model
# 3. Extract Feature Maps from a Specific Layer. IMPORTANT
STEP!
layer_name = 'layer1'  # Choose the layer to visualize
feature_maps = []

def get_feature_maps(name):
    def hook(model, input, output):
        feature_maps.append(output.detach()) #Gets the output
    return hook #Returns a function to be used.

for name, module in resnet18.named_modules():
    if name == layer_name:
        module.register_forward_hook(get_feature_maps(name))

# 4. Run the Image Through the Model: Extract the features
output = resnet18(input_batch) #This will also automatically
fill the "feature_maps"

# 5. Visualize the Feature Maps with Matplotlib.
feature_map = feature_maps[0]  #Gets the images to visualize.

num_channels = feature_map.shape[1]  #Gets the Channels
num_cols = 8                          #Number of cols for
output
num_rows = num_channels // num_cols + 1  #Calculates the
number of rows

fig, axes = plt.subplots(num_rows, num_cols, figsize=(12,
12)) #Configures the size

for i in range(num_channels):
    row = i // num_cols
    col = i % num_cols
    ax = axes[row, col] if num_rows > 1 else axes[col]
#Handles whether there's multiple images to show or just one
    img = feature_map[0, i, :, :].cpu().numpy() #Sets the
image to view. Gets the dimensions correct
    ax.imshow(img, cmap='viridis') #Chooses the type.
    ax.axis('off') #Turn off numbers.
```

```
plt.show()
```

Walking through the Code:

1. **Loading Pre-trained Model:** We load a pre-trained ResNet-18 model from torchvision.models.
2. **Image Preprocessing:** We load and preprocess the image using the same transformations that were used to train the pre-trained model.
3. **Extract Feature Maps:** The real magic happens here. We use a "forward hook" to extract the output of a specific layer in the network. The register_forward_hook function allows you to execute a custom function every time the specified layer is called during the forward pass.
4. **Pass Through the Model:** Run the preprocessed image through the resnet. This will also automatically trigger the forward hook as well.
5. **Visualization:** We iterate over the feature maps and display them as grayscale images using Matplotlib. Higher activation values are represented by brighter colors.

Personal Insight: One of my favorite things to do is visualize the feature maps of a CNN after it has been trained. It's like discovering what parts of the image the model values as important.

Interpreting Feature Maps:

- **Early Layers:** Feature maps in the early layers of the network typically represent low-level features like edges, corners, and textures.
- **Later Layers:** Feature maps in the later layers tend to represent higher-level features like object parts and entire objects.
- **Strong Activations:** Feature maps with strong activations indicate that the corresponding filter is detecting a relevant pattern in the input image.

More Advanced Techniques: Gradient-Based Methods

More sophisticated techniques like Gradient-weighted Class Activation Mapping (Grad-CAM) use the gradients of the output class with respect to the feature maps to highlight the regions of the input image that are most relevant to the model's prediction. This provides a more localized and interpretable visualization.

Conclusion

Visualizing feature maps is a powerful technique for understanding how CNNs process images and for debugging and improving your models. By exploring these internal representations, you can gain valuable insights into the inner workings of these complex networks. Visualizing allows you to see just what the models are learning and adapting to in ways that metrics alone simply cannot convey. Let's see how we can use this to our advantage with the final section.

6.4 Best Practices for Image Classification: Maximizing Performance - Achieving Top-Tier Results

Image classification is a highly competitive field, and achieving state-of-the-art results requires more than just a basic understanding of CNN architectures. This section will outline the essential best practices for building high-performance image classifiers, guiding you through the crucial steps that can make the difference between a mediocre model and a champion. Think of this as a masterclass in image classification, revealing the secrets and techniques used by the world's leading researchers and practitioners.

Why Best Practices Matter: Following these guidelines will help you:

- Build more accurate and robust image classifiers.
- Train your models more efficiently.
- Prevent overfitting and improve generalization performance.
- Effectively debug and troubleshoot your models.

1. Data Preparation: The Foundation of Success

- **Collect a Diverse and Representative Dataset:** Your dataset should accurately reflect the real-world distribution of images that your model will encounter. Ensure that you have sufficient data for each class and that the data is diverse enough to capture the variations within each class.
- **Clean and Label Your Data:** Carefully review your data and correct any errors or inconsistencies in the labels. This is a time-consuming but essential step.
- **Split Your Data Properly:** Divide your data into training, validation, and test sets. The validation set is used to tune your

hyperparameters and prevent overfitting, while the test set is used to evaluate the final performance of your model. The data from each should be as similar as possible.

2. Choosing the Right Architecture: A Balancing Act

- **Start with Pre-trained Models:** Transfer learning is your friend. Leverage pre-trained models whenever possible, especially when you have limited data. Models such as ResNet, VGG, and EfficientNet are well documented in TorchVision.
- **Consider Your Task and Resources:** Select an architecture that is appropriate for the complexity of your task and the available computational resources. Deeper and more complex architectures can achieve higher accuracy but require more training time and memory.
- **Experiment with Different Architectures:** Don't be afraid to experiment with different architectures to find what works best for your specific problem.

3. Data Augmentation: Expanding Your Horizons

- **Apply Relevant Transformations:** Choose augmentation techniques that are representative of the real-world variations that your model will encounter. For example, if you're training a model to recognize objects in images taken from different camera angles, use random rotations.
- **Be Careful Not to Introduce Unrealistic Artifacts:** Avoid transformations that are not realistic or could introduce artifacts into your data. For example, flipping images upside down might not be appropriate for many tasks.
- **Tune the Augmentation Intensity:** Experiment with different augmentation intensities to find what works best. Too little augmentation may not be enough to prevent overfitting, while too much augmentation can degrade performance.

4. Training Your Model: Finding the Optimal Parameters

- **Choose an Appropriate Optimizer:** Adam and RMSprop are good starting points for many problems. If your model is overfitting, consider using SGD with momentum.
- **Tune Your Learning Rate:** The learning rate is a critical hyperparameter that controls the step size taken during each update of the model's parameters. Experiment with different learning rate

schedules and adaptive learning rate methods to find what works best. Tools such as ReduceLROnPlateau can help with the tuning.

- **Use Batch Normalization:** Batch normalization can significantly improve training stability and convergence speed, especially in deep networks.
- **Regularize Your Model:** Use dropout and weight decay to prevent overfitting. The choice for weight decay will depend on the optimizer that you are using, such as Adam.
- **Monitor Your Metrics:** Track the performance of your model on the training and validation sets to monitor overfitting and adjust your hyperparameters accordingly.
- **Implement Early Stopping:** Stop training when the validation performance starts to degrade.
- **Use torch.compile:** (dynamo) is very useful out of the box for performance increases. If compatible, implement.

5. Evaluation: Measuring Your Success

- **Use Appropriate Metrics:** Don't rely solely on accuracy. Use metrics like precision, recall, F1-score, and AUC-ROC to get a more complete picture of your model's performance, especially when dealing with imbalanced datasets.
- **Evaluate on a Held-Out Test Set:** Evaluate the final performance of your model on a held-out test set that was not used during training or validation. This will give you an unbiased estimate of the model's generalization performance.

Code Examples:

Many of these steps have code examples already in other chapters! Here is how you would put it all together.

```python
import torch
import torch.nn as nn
import torch.optim as optim
from torchvision import models, transforms
from torch.utils.data import DataLoader, Dataset
from PIL import Image
import os

# 1. Data Preparation

# Create datasets and dataloaders using custom Dataset and
DataLoader classes
```

```python
# 2. Choose Pre-Trained
model_ft = models.resnet18(pretrained=True)
num_ftrs = model_ft.fc.in_features
model_ft.fc = nn.Linear(num_ftrs, num_classes)  # num_classes
is the final class size

# 3. Loss, optimizer, and LR Scheduler
criterion = nn.CrossEntropyLoss(weight=class_weights)  # If
class weights exist.
optimizer_ft = optim.Adam(model_ft.parameters(), lr=0.001,
weight_decay=0.001)

# 4. Implement Data Agumentation with Dataset and
transformations
image = Image.open(image_path).convert('RGB')

transform = transforms.Compose([ #Transform data
    transforms.Resize(256),
    transforms.RandomHorizontalFlip(),
    transforms.ToTensor(),
    transforms.Normalize(mean=[0.485, 0.456, 0.406],
std=[0.229, 0.224, 0.225])
])

# 5. Implement Training
#Run the model
def train_model(model, criterion, optimizer, scheduler,
num_epochs=2): #This was a previous function from an earlier
chapter

        #Each epoch has a training and validation phase
        for phase in ['train', 'test']:
            if phase == 'train':
                model.train()  #Set model to training mode
            else:
                model.eval() #Set model to evaluate mode

            running_loss = 0.0
            running_corrects = 0

            #Iterate over data.
            for inputs, labels in dataloaders[phase]:

                #Zero the parameter gradients
                optimizer.zero_grad()

                #forward
                with torch.set_grad_enabled(phase ==
'train'): #Only track in train step
                    outputs = model(inputs) #Get output
```

```
                    _, preds = torch.max(outputs, 1) #Predict
output
                    loss = criterion(outputs, labels)
#Calculate Loss

                    #backward + optimize only if in training
phase
                    if phase == 'train':
                        loss.backward()  #Back Propagate
                        optimizer.step() #Optimizer

                #statistics
                running_loss += loss.item() * inputs.size(0)
#Track loss
                running_corrects += torch.sum(preds ==
labels.data) #Compare preditions to labels

            if phase == 'train':
                scheduler.step() #Decay learning rate at the
END of every training phase!

            epoch_loss = running_loss / dataset_sizes[phase]
#Report results
            epoch_acc = running_corrects.double() /
dataset_sizes[phase] #Report results

            print('Epoch is complete {} Phase: {} Loss:
{:.4f} Acc: {:.4f}'.format(epoch, phase, epoch_loss,
epoch_acc))

# 6. Evaluate

evalModel = train_model(model_ft, criterion, optimizer_ft,
exp_lr_scheduler, num_epochs=2) #Load trained model and see
what its results are
print(f"Final evaluation performance on image = {evalModel}")
```

Personal Insight: I've learned that meticulous data preparation and careful hyperparameter tuning are essential for achieving state-of-the-art results in image classification. Don't underestimate the importance of these steps.

Conclusion

By following these best practices, you can build high-performance image classifiers that are accurate, robust, and generalizable. Keep these best practices in mind as you apply them to various challenges. These key

components are the best way to unlock superior results in your models!
Great job so far!

Chapter 7: Natural Language Processing with RNNs and Transformers - Giving Machines the Gift of Language

Natural Language Processing (NLP) has made tremendous strides in recent years, enabling machines to understand, interpret, and generate human language with remarkable fluency. This chapter will guide you through the core concepts and techniques of NLP, focusing on Recurrent Neural Networks (RNNs) and Transformers, two of the most influential architectures in the field. Prepare to unlock the power of language for your models.

Why NLP with RNNs and Transformers Matters: These techniques allow you to build models that can perform a wide range of NLP tasks, such as text classification, machine translation, sentiment analysis, and text generation.

7.1 RNNs: LSTMs, GRUs, and Sequence Modeling - Processing the Flow of Language: Decoding the Secrets of Sequential Data

Recurrent Neural Networks (RNNs) represent a fundamental shift from the static processing of feedforward networks to the dynamic handling of sequential data. They're designed to process sequences of information, such as text, audio, or time series, by maintaining an internal memory of past inputs. This ability to "remember" past information makes them particularly well-suited for tasks where the order of the data matters, like understanding the meaning of a sentence or predicting the next note in a musical composition.

Why Understanding RNNs Matters: RNNs are the foundation for many advanced NLP techniques and remain useful today. They provide a stepping stone for grasping the more complicated Transformer model.

Unrolling Time: Processing Sequences Step-by-Step

The core idea behind RNNs is to process the input sequence one element at a time, updating an internal *hidden state* at each step. This hidden state acts as a memory, capturing information about the past elements of the sequence.

- **Time Steps:** The sequential processing of inputs, where each input element is processed at a specific point in time.
- **Hidden State (ht):** The internal memory of the RNN, which is updated at each time step.
- **Input (xt):** The current element being processed at time step t.
- **Recurrent Connection:** The feedback connection that allows the hidden state to be passed from one time step to the next.

The Vanishing Gradient Problem: A Hurdle in RNN Training

Traditional RNNs, also known as "vanilla RNNs," suffer from a significant limitation: the vanishing gradient problem. This occurs when the gradients used to update the network's weights become very small as they are backpropagated through time, making it difficult for the network to learn long-range dependencies. It essentially "forgets" what came before!

LSTM (Long Short-Term Memory): Remembering the Past

LSTMs were designed to address the vanishing gradient problem by introducing a more complex memory cell with gates that control the flow of information into and out of the cell. These gates allow the LSTM to selectively remember relevant information and forget irrelevant information, making it better at capturing long-range dependencies.

Key Components of an LSTM Cell:

- **Cell State (Ct):** The core of the LSTM, representing the long-term memory of the network.
- **Forget Gate (ft):** Determines which information to discard from the cell state.
- **Input Gate (it):** Determines which new information to add to the cell state.
- **Output Gate (ot):** Determines which information to output from the cell state.

GRU (Gated Recurrent Unit): A Simplified Approach

GRUs are a simplified version of LSTMs with fewer parameters, making them faster to train and less prone to overfitting. They combine the cell state and hidden state into a single state vector and use two gates:

- **Reset Gate (rt):** Determines how much of the past hidden state to forget.
- **Update Gate (zt):** Determines how much of the new input to incorporate into the hidden state.

```python
import torch
import torch.nn as nn

# Example: Creating an LSTM and GRU in PyTorch

# 1. LSTM
lstm = nn.LSTM(input_size=10, hidden_size=20, num_layers=2,
batch_first=True) #Multi-layer, with batch size
print(f"LSTM:\n{lstm}")

# 2. GRU
gru = nn.GRU(input_size=10, hidden_size=20, num_layers=2,
batch_first=True)
print(f"GRU:\n{gru}")

#Sample input
sample_input = torch.randn(5, 3, 10) #Batch size 5, Sequence
length 3, Feature size 10

# Pass through LSTM and GRU
output_lstm, (h_n, c_n)  = lstm(sample_input)
print(f"LSTM Output: {output_lstm.shape}") #Shape is
[5,3,20], since input_size is 10
print(f"LSTM Hidden: {h_n.shape}") #Shape is [2,5,20], since
num_layers is 2, batch_size is 5 and hidden is 2

output_gru, h_n = gru(sample_input) #Only one hidden output
print(f"GRU Output: {output_gru.shape}") #Shape is [5,3,20],
since input_size is 10
print(f"GRU Hidden: {h_n.shape}") #Shape is [2,5,20], since
num_layers is 2, batch_size is 5 and hidden is 2
```

Practical Explanation:

- The input_size parameter specifies the number of features in the input sequence.
- The hidden_size parameter specifies the number of hidden units in the RNN.
- The num_layers parameter specifies the number of layers in the RNN.
- The batch_first parameter specifies whether the input data should have the batch size as the first dimension (recommended).

114

Output Details:

- The output of the LSTM and GRU modules has shape (batch_size, sequence_length, hidden_size). This represents the hidden state at each time step.
- The final hidden state has shape (num_layers, batch_size, hidden_size). This represents the final state of the RNN after processing the entire sequence.
- The LSTM also returns the final cell state, which has the same shape as the final hidden state.

Sequence Modeling Tasks: Putting RNNs to Work

RNNs can be used for a wide range of sequence modeling tasks, including:

- **Text Classification:** Classifying text into different categories (e.g., sentiment analysis, spam detection). The RNN processes the text sequence and outputs a single vector representation, which is then fed into a classifier.
- **Machine Translation:** Translating text from one language to another. The RNN processes the input sentence and generates the corresponding translation in the target language.
- **Text Generation:** Generating new text based on a given prompt or context. The RNN predicts the next word in the sequence, and the process is repeated to generate longer sequences of text.

Personal Insight: I've used LSTMs for sentiment analysis and found them to be very effective at capturing the nuances of human language. The ability to remember past words in a sentence is crucial for understanding the overall sentiment.

Conclusion

RNNs, particularly LSTMs and GRUs, are a powerful tool for modeling sequential data. By understanding the underlying concepts and how to implement them in PyTorch, you can effectively tackle a wide range of NLP tasks. They also form the basis for the more advanced networks that we will be using next!

7.2 Word Embeddings and Pre-trained Language Models (BERT, etc.) - Representing the Meaning of Words: Bridging the Gap Between Language and Machines

To enable machines to truly understand and process human language, we need to find a way to represent words in a format that captures their semantic meaning. This is where word embeddings and pre-trained language models come into play. These techniques transform words into dense vectors that encode the relationships between words, allowing machines to reason about language in a more sophisticated way. They're like creating a universal translator that allows humans and machines to communicate seamlessly.

Why Word Embeddings and Pre-trained Language Models Matter: These techniques are essential for:

- Capturing the semantic meaning of words.
- Improving the performance of NLP models on a wide range of tasks.
- Leveraging pre-trained knowledge to reduce the need for large, labeled datasets.

From One-Hot Encoding to Dense Vectors: A Shift in Representation

Traditional approaches to representing words, such as one-hot encoding, suffer from several limitations. One-hot encoding creates a sparse vector for each word, where all elements are zero except for a single element that corresponds to the word's index in the vocabulary. This approach is simple, but it doesn't capture any semantic relationships between words and can be inefficient for large vocabularies.

Word embeddings offer a more effective alternative. They represent words as dense vectors in a continuous vector space, where words with similar meanings are located closer together. This allows the model to capture semantic relationships between words and to generalize to unseen words based on their proximity to known words.

Key Concepts:

- **Vocabulary:** The set of all unique words in your dataset.
- **Embedding Dimension:** The size of the dense vector used to represent each word.

- **Semantic Similarity:** The degree to which two words have similar meanings.

Practical Implementation: Let's say we have a small vocabulary consisting of ["king", "queen", "man", "woman", "apple"]. One-hot-encoding is:

- King: [1, 0, 0, 0, 0]
- Queen: [0, 1, 0, 0, 0]
- Man: [0, 0, 1, 0, 0]
- Woman: [0, 0, 0, 1, 0]
- Apple: [0, 0, 0, 0, 1]

With word embeddings, you can use values such as:

- King: [0.9, 0.2, 0.1, 0.3]
- Queen: [0.8, 0.3, 0.2, 0.2]
- Man: [0.2, 0.9, 0.3, 0.1]
- Woman: [0.3, 0.7, 0.2, 0.2]
- Apple: [0.1, 0.1, 0.9, 0.8]

The values will vary based on the network. Note that "king" and "queen" and "man" and "woman" have values that are close to each other.

Word2Vec and GloVe: Learning Word Embeddings from Scratch

Word2Vec and GloVe are two popular algorithms for learning word embeddings from scratch. These algorithms are trained on large text corpora and learn to predict the context of a word (Word2Vec) or to capture the co-occurrence statistics of words (GloVe).

- **Word2Vec:**
    - *Continuous Bag-of-Words (CBOW):* Predicts a target word based on its surrounding context words.
    - *Skip-gram:* Predicts the surrounding context words based on a target word.
- *GloVe (Global Vectors for Word Representation):*
    - Learns word embeddings by factorizing a matrix of word co-occurrence statistics.

Pre-trained Language Models: Unleashing Contextual Understanding

Pre-trained language models (PLMs) have revolutionized NLP by providing a way to capture the contextual meaning of words. Unlike Word2Vec and GloVe, which assign a single embedding vector to each word, PLMs generate contextualized embeddings that depend on the surrounding words in the sentence. This allows the model to capture the nuances of language and to better understand the meaning of words in different contexts.

- **BERT (Bidirectional Encoder Representations from Transformers):**
    - A powerful PLM that captures bidirectional contextual information by training on two tasks: masked language modeling and next sentence prediction.
- **GPT (Generative Pre-trained Transformer):**
    - A powerful PLM designed for text generation. It captures unidirectional contextual information by training on a language modeling task.

```python
import torch
import torch.nn as nn

# 1. Using PyTorch's Embedding Layer
embedding = nn.Embedding(num_embeddings=10000,
embedding_dim=300) # vocab_size is 1000, embed_dim is 300
print(f"Embedding Layer:\n{embedding}") #Embedding

# Look up embedding vector of word "2"
word_index = torch.tensor([2]) #Word that we're looking for
embedding_vector = embedding(word_index)

print(f"The embedding vector for word {word_index} is
\n{embedding_vector.shape}") #Shape is [1,300]

# 2. Using Hugging Face Transformers (BERT)
from transformers import BertTokenizer, BertModel

# Load pre-trained model and tokenizer
tokenizer = BertTokenizer.from_pretrained('bert-base-
uncased')
model = BertModel.from_pretrained('bert-base-uncased')

# Process input text
text = "Here is the sentence I want embeddings for."
inputs = tokenizer(text, return_tensors="pt") #Returns tensor
object

with torch.no_grad():
```

```
    outputs = model(**inputs) #Passes the inputs to get
outputs
    last_hidden_states = outputs.last_hidden_state

#The first value is the embedding for the word.
print(f"Bert's embedding for sample sentence is
{last_hidden_states.shape}") #768 is the embedding dimension.
[1, 9, 768]
```

Implementation Notes:

- When using PyTorch's nn.Embedding layer, you need to create a vocabulary and assign an index to each word in your dataset. You can then use these indices to look up the corresponding embedding vectors.
- When using Hugging Face Transformers, the tokenizer handles the vocabulary and tokenization process for you. You simply provide the input text, and the tokenizer will convert it into a format that can be fed into the pre-trained language model.

Personal Insight: I've found that pre-trained language models like BERT and GPT significantly improve the performance of NLP models, especially when you have limited data. The ability to capture the contextual meaning of words is crucial for many NLP tasks.

Conclusion

Word embeddings and pre-trained language models are essential tools for bridging the gap between human language and machines. They provide a powerful way to represent the meaning of words, allowing machines to understand, interpret, and generate human language with unprecedented fluency. By mastering these techniques, you'll be well-equipped to tackle a wide range of NLP challenges. Are you ready to explore Transformers next?

7.3 Transformers: Architecture and Implementation - The Rise of Attention: A Paradigm Shift in Sequence Modeling

The Transformer architecture has revolutionized the field of Natural Language Processing (NLP), surpassing Recurrent Neural Networks (RNNs) in many tasks and becoming the foundation for state-of-the-art language models like BERT and GPT. Unlike RNNs, Transformers don't rely on recurrent connections to process sequential data. Instead, they use a powerful mechanism called "attention" to weigh the importance of different parts of the input sequence when making predictions. Think of them as having unlimited memory that they can selectively access, allowing them to capture long-range dependencies with remarkable effectiveness.

Why Understanding Transformers Matters: Transformers are the dominant architecture in NLP today. Understanding their architecture and implementation is essential for building and using state-of-the-art language models.

Breaking Down the Transformer: A Modular Approach

The Transformer architecture consists of several key components, each contributing to its overall power and flexibility:

- **Self-Attention:** The heart of the Transformer. It allows the model to attend to different parts of the *same* input sequence, capturing relationships between words regardless of their distance in the sequence.
- **Multi-Head Attention:** Extends the self-attention mechanism by using multiple "attention heads" in parallel. Each attention head learns a different set of attention weights, allowing the model to capture different aspects of the relationships between words.
- **Encoder:** Processes the input sequence and learns a contextualized representation. It consists of multiple layers, each containing a self-attention module and a feedforward network.
- **Decoder:** Generates the output sequence (e.g., in machine translation). It also consists of multiple layers, each containing a self-attention module, an encoder-decoder attention module (which attends to the output of the encoder), and a feedforward network.
- **Positional Encoding:** Since Transformers don't have recurrent connections, they need a way to encode the position of words in the input sequence. Positional encodings are added to the word embeddings to provide this information.

Self-Attention: Focusing on the Relevant Parts

The self-attention mechanism is the key innovation that enables Transformers to capture long-range dependencies. It works by computing a weighted sum of the input embeddings, where the weights are determined by the attention scores. The attention scores indicate the relevance of each word in the input sequence to the current word being processed.

The Self-Attention Formula:

Attention(Q, K, V) = softmax((QK^T) / sqrt(dk))V

Where:

- Q (Query): A matrix representing the word being "queried" for relevant connections.
- K (Key): A matrix representing all words in the input sequence, used to compute attention scores.
- V (Value): A matrix representing all words in the input sequence, used to compute the weighted sum.
- dk: The dimension of the key vectors (used for scaling).

Putting It All Together: Using Hugging Face Transformers

While implementing a Transformer from scratch can be a complex undertaking, the Hugging Face Transformers library provides a convenient way to use pre-trained Transformer models and build custom models on top of them.

```python
import torch
import torch.nn as nn
from transformers import BertModel, BertTokenizer

class TransformerClassifier(nn.Module):
    def __init__(self, num_classes):
        super(TransformerClassifier, self).__init__()
        self.bert = BertModel.from_pretrained('bert-base-uncased') #Loads the pretrained
        self.dropout = nn.Dropout(0.1) #Dropout Layer, to reduce Overfitting.
        self.linear = nn.Linear(768, num_classes)  # Adjust input size

    def forward(self, input_ids, attention_mask):
        outputs = self.bert(input_ids=input_ids, attention_mask=attention_mask) #Get bert layers.
        pooled_output = outputs.pooler_output #Final layers

        x = self.dropout(pooled_output)
        x = self.linear(x) #Now set it up for your dimensions.

        return x
```

```
# Example Usage:
num_classes = 2 #Number of classes to predict

model = TransformerClassifier(num_classes)

#Sample Code
from transformers import BertTokenizer
tokenizer = BertTokenizer.from_pretrained('bert-base-
uncased') #Load the specific pretrained tokenizer.

#Process into Tensors
text = "Insert a long paragraph here to process"
inputs = tokenizer(text, return_tensors="pt", padding=True,
truncation=True) #If over dimension, truncate.

#Pass the inputs.
outputs = model(inputs['input_ids'],
inputs['attention_mask']) #Pass it
print(outputs)
```

Key Improvements and Clarifications:

- **Custom Classifier:** It now includes an example of how to fine-tune it with your own linear layer, which is normally what you want.
- **Truncation:** Uses truncation to resolve the problems with very long chains.
- **Padding:** Uses padding, which also helps resolve problems.

Walking through the Code:

1. **Load Pre-trained Model and Tokenizer:** We load a pre-trained BERT model and tokenizer from the Hugging Face Transformers library.
2. **Process Input Text:** We use the tokenizer to convert the input text into a format that can be fed into the BERT model. This involves tokenizing the text, adding special tokens (e.g., [CLS] and [SEP]), and padding or truncating the sequence to a fixed length.
3. **Pass Input to Model:** We pass the tokenized input to the BERT model to obtain the contextualized embeddings.

Personal Insight: The Hugging Face Transformers library has made it incredibly easy to use and fine-tune pre-trained Transformer models. It's a valuable tool for any NLP practitioner.

Conclusion

Transformers have revolutionized the field of NLP, achieving state-of-the-art results on a wide range of tasks. While the architecture can seem complex at first, understanding the underlying concepts of self-attention and multi-head attention will enable you to effectively use and adapt these models for your own NLP projects. By using HuggingFace, this has become remarkably easy, allowing you to work with prebuilt models without constructing the more complex network elements! And with that, we will move onto another type of neural network: GANs!

Chapter 8: Generative Adversarial Networks (GANs) - The Art of Creating New Realities

Generative Adversarial Networks (GANs) have emerged as a powerful class of neural networks capable of generating new, realistic data samples. Unlike discriminative models that learn to classify data, GANs learn to *create* data that resembles the training data. Think of this chapter as learning to be an artist, capable of creating new images, music, or text that mimics the style of a master.

Why GANs Matter: GANs have a wide range of applications, including:

- Image generation (creating new images from scratch).
- Image editing (modifying existing images in realistic ways).
- Style transfer (transferring the style of one image to another).
- Data augmentation (generating synthetic data to improve the performance of other models).
- Generating text, music, and other types of data.

8.1 GAN Fundamentals: Generator and Discriminator - The Dueling Networks: Two Minds, One Goal

At the heart of every Generative Adversarial Network (GAN) lies a fascinating interplay between two neural networks: the Generator and the Discriminator. These networks are trained simultaneously in a competitive game, pushing each other to improve and ultimately leading to the generation of new, realistic data samples. Think of it as a creative collaboration, where two artists challenge each other to create ever-more-compelling works.

Why Understand the Generator and Discriminator? Understanding the roles and responsibilities of the generator and discriminator is crucial for:

- Designing effective GAN architectures.
- Troubleshooting training instability.
- Controlling the quality and diversity of the generated data.

The Generator: The Artist of the GAN

The generator takes random noise as input and transforms it into synthetic data samples. Its goal is to learn the underlying distribution of the real data and to create samples that are indistinguishable from the real thing. In essence, the generator is like an artist who is trying to create realistic paintings that can fool art critics.

Key Aspects of the Generator:

- **Input:** A random noise vector (often drawn from a normal distribution). This noise provides the source of randomness for generating diverse samples.
- **Architecture:** Typically a feedforward neural network (often with transposed convolutional layers for image generation). The architecture should be designed to transform the random noise into data samples that have the same dimensions and characteristics as the real data.
- **Output:** Synthetic data samples that are intended to resemble the real data. The output layer typically uses an activation function that matches the range of the real data (e.g., Tanh for images in the range [-1, 1]).

The Discriminator: The Art Critic of the GAN

The discriminator takes both real data samples and synthetic data samples generated by the generator as input and tries to distinguish between them. Its goal is to correctly classify real data as real and synthetic data as fake. Think of it as an art critic who is trying to identify fake paintings and expose the forger.

Key Aspects of the Discriminator:

- **Input:** Both real data samples and synthetic data samples generated by the generator.
- **Architecture:** Typically a feedforward neural network (often with convolutional layers for image classification). The architecture should be designed to extract features from the input data and classify it as either real or fake.
- **Output:** A probability score between 0 and 1, indicating the likelihood that the input data is real.

The Adversarial Training Process: A Dynamic Equilibrium

The generator and discriminator are trained simultaneously in an alternating fashion. The generator tries to fool the discriminator, while the discriminator tries to catch the generator. This adversarial process drives both networks to improve their performance, resulting in a generator that can generate increasingly realistic data samples.

Training Steps:

1. **Train the Discriminator:**
   - Sample a batch of real data samples from the training set.
   - Generate a batch of synthetic data samples using the generator.
   - Train the discriminator to correctly classify real data as real and synthetic data as fake.
2. **Train the Generator:**
   - Generate a batch of synthetic data samples using the generator.
   - Train the generator to generate samples that the discriminator classifies as real.

Personal Insight: I find the adversarial training process to be a very elegant and intuitive way to train generative models. The competition between the generator and discriminator pushes both networks to improve their performance, resulting in the generation of high-quality data samples.

Loss Functions: Guiding the Training Process

The training process is driven by two loss functions:

- **Discriminator Loss:** Measures how well the discriminator can distinguish between real and synthetic data.

  *For a real data point x, D(x) is what the Discriminator outputs. The correct value, according to the loss function, should be 1. Hence the function name, "real_loss"

  For a generated data point G(z), D(G(z)) is what the Discriminator outputs. The correct value, according to the loss function, should be 0. Hence the function name, "fake_loss"

```
real_loss = criterion(discriminator(real_data),
torch.ones(batch_size, 1))
```

```
fake_loss = criterion(discriminator(generator(noise)),
torch.zeros(batch_size, 1))
discriminator_loss = (real_loss + fake_loss) / 2
```

- **Generator Loss:** Measures how well the generator can fool the discriminator. The correct value, according to the loss function, should be 1.

  For a generated data point G(z), D(G(z)) is what the Discriminator outputs. The generator wants the result to be evaluated at 1. Hence the function name, "generator_loss"

```
generator_loss =
criterion(discriminator(generator(noise)),
torch.ones(batch_size, 1))
```

Putting It All Together: A Minimal Example in PyTorch

```python
import torch
import torch.nn as nn
import torch.optim as optim

# Example: Building a simple GAN

# 1. Define the Generator
class Generator(nn.Module):
    def __init__(self, latent_dim, output_dim):
        super(Generator, self).__init__()
        self.model = nn.Sequential(
            nn.Linear(latent_dim, 128),
            nn.ReLU(),
            nn.Linear(128, output_dim),
            nn.Tanh()   # Output range [-1, 1]
        )

    def forward(self, z):
        output = self.model(z)
        return output

# 2. Define the Discriminator
class Discriminator(nn.Module):
    def __init__(self, input_dim):
        super(Discriminator, self).__init__()
        self.model = nn.Sequential(
            nn.Linear(input_dim, 128),
            nn.ReLU(),
```

```python
            nn.Linear(128, 1),
            nn.Sigmoid() # Output range [0, 1]
        )

    def forward(self, x):
        output = self.model(x)
        return output

# 3. Hyperparameters
latent_dim = 64
image_dim = 784  # For MNIST (28x28)
lr = 0.0002
batch_size = 128
num_epochs = 50

# 4. Instantiate the Generator and Discriminator
generator = Generator(latent_dim, image_dim)
discriminator = Discriminator(image_dim)

# 5. Define the Optimizers
optimizer_G = optim.Adam(generator.parameters(), lr=lr)
optimizer_D = optim.Adam(discriminator.parameters(), lr=lr)

# 6. Loss Function
criterion = nn.BCELoss() #Binary cross entropy loss

#Sample training. normally done in image loaders.
real_data = torch.randn(batch_size, image_dim) #Instead load
from a dataset.
noise = torch.randn(batch_size, latent_dim) #Generate Noise

# 7. Train the GAN
for epoch in range(num_epochs):
    #7a. Generate batch
    noise = torch.randn(batch_size, latent_dim) #Generate
Noise

    # 7b: TRAIN DISCRIMINATOR: max log(D(real)) + log(1 -
D(G(z)))
    real_loss = criterion(discriminator(real_data),
torch.ones(batch_size, 1))
    fake_loss = criterion(discriminator(generator(noise)),
torch.zeros(batch_size, 1))
    discriminator_loss = (real_loss + fake_loss) / 2 #Average
the results.

    #Back Propogate with optimizers
    optimizer_D.zero_grad()   #Reset gradients before each
pass
    discriminator_loss.backward()
    optimizer_D.step()
```

```
    # 7c. TRAIN GENERATOR: min log(1 - D(G(z))) <-> max
log(D(G(z))
    generator_loss =
criterion(discriminator(generator(noise)),
torch.ones(batch_size, 1)) #Pass though discriminator.
    optimizer_G.zero_grad()    #Reset gradients before each
pass
    generator_loss.backward() #Calculate new.
    optimizer_G.step()

    #Report out results
    if epoch % 10 == 0:
        print(f"Epoch [{epoch}/{num_epochs}] Loss D:
{discriminator_loss:.4f}, loss G: {generator_loss:.4f}")
```

Personal Insight: Training GANs can be tricky. The adversarial training process can be unstable, and it's often difficult to find the right balance between the generator and discriminator. Monitoring the loss functions and generated samples carefully is essential for successful training.

Conclusion

Understanding the roles and responsibilities of the generator and discriminator is fundamental to working with GANs. By mastering the adversarial training process and carefully designing the architectures of these two networks, you can unlock the creative potential of GANs and generate new, realistic data samples. This creates an exciting and challenging area of machine learning! Are you ready to continue exploring this subject?

8.2 GAN Variants: DCGAN, WGAN, and Conditional GANs - Expanding the GAN Family: Taming Instability and Adding Control

The original GAN architecture, while groundbreaking, suffers from several limitations, including training instability and a lack of control over the generated data. To address these challenges, numerous GAN variants have been developed, each building upon the foundations of the original GAN to improve its performance and capabilities. This section will explore three of the most influential GAN variants: DCGAN, WGAN, and Conditional GANs, showcasing how they tackle these limitations and unlock new possibilities.

Why Explore GAN Variants? Understanding these variants is crucial for:

- Building more stable and reliable GAN models.
- Generating higher-quality and more diverse data samples.
- Controlling the characteristics of the generated data.
- Adapting GANs to specific tasks and datasets.

DCGAN (Deep Convolutional GAN): Merging CNNs with GANs

DCGANs (Deep Convolutional GANs) combine the power of Convolutional Neural Networks (CNNs) with the adversarial training framework of GANs. This architecture replaces the fully connected layers of the original GAN with convolutional layers in both the generator and discriminator, making it particularly well-suited for generating realistic images.

Key Improvements in DCGANs:

- **Convolutional Layers:** Using convolutional layers allows the generator and discriminator to learn spatial hierarchies of features, leading to the generation of more realistic images.
- **Batch Normalization:** Using batch normalization in both the generator and discriminator improves training stability and allows for higher learning rates.
- **No Pooling Layers:** Removing pooling layers helps to preserve spatial information and prevent the loss of fine-grained details.
- **ReLU and Leaky ReLU Activations:** Using ReLU activation functions in the generator (except for the output layer, which uses Tanh) and Leaky ReLU activation functions in the discriminator improves training stability and gradient flow.
- **Strided and Transposed Convolutions:** Using strided convolutions in the discriminator for downsampling and transposed convolutions in the generator for upsampling allows the networks to learn the appropriate spatial transformations.

WGAN (Wasserstein GAN): A More Stable Training Signal

WGANs (Wasserstein GANs) address the training instability issues of traditional GANs by using the Wasserstein distance (also known as the Earth Mover's distance) as a loss function. The Wasserstein distance provides a smoother and more informative training signal than the traditional GAN loss, leading to more stable training and improved sample quality.

Key Improvements in WGANs:

- **Wasserstein Distance:** Using the Wasserstein distance as a loss function provides a more robust and stable training signal.
- **Weight Clipping:** Clipping the weights of the discriminator to enforce a Lipschitz constraint helps to ensure that the Wasserstein distance is well-defined and prevents the discriminator from becoming too powerful.
- **Linear Activation Function:** Using a linear activation function in the discriminator (instead of Sigmoid) avoids saturation and improves gradient flow.

Conditional GANs (cGANs): Adding Control to the Generation Process

Conditional GANs (cGANs) allow you to control the type of data that the generator generates by providing additional information (e.g., class labels, text descriptions) as input to both the generator and discriminator. This allows you to generate data samples with specific characteristics or attributes.

Key Concepts in cGANs:

- **Conditional Input:** Providing additional information (e.g., class labels, text descriptions) as input to both the generator and discriminator.
- **Concatenation:** Concatenating the conditional input with the random noise in the generator and with the data sample in the discriminator.

Let's dive into the code and see how to implement different GAN variations with PyTorch

```
    import torch
import torch.nn as nn

#Basic Conditional GAN
class ConditionalGenerator(nn.Module):
    def __init__(self, latent_dim, num_classes, output_dim):
        super(ConditionalGenerator, self).__init__()
        self.label_embedding = nn.Embedding(num_classes,
latent_dim) #Embed labels
        self.model = nn.Sequential(
            nn.Linear(latent_dim * 2, 128),   # Input is noise
+ label embedding
            nn.ReLU(),
```

```python
            nn.Linear(128, output_dim),
            nn.Tanh()
        )
    def forward(self, noise, labels):
        #Combine labels with a One-Hot Vector or anything
else.
        label_embed = self.label_embedding(labels)
        combined_input = torch.cat((noise, label_embed),
dim=-1)
        output = self.model(combined_input)
        return output

# Discriminator
class ConditionalDiscriminator(nn.Module):
    def __init__(self, input_dim, num_classes):
        super(ConditionalDiscriminator, self).__init__()
        self.label_embedding = nn.Embedding(num_classes,
input_dim) #Embed labels
        self.model = nn.Sequential(
            nn.Linear(input_dim * 2, 128),   # Input is image
+ label embedding
            nn.LeakyReLU(0.2),
            nn.Linear(128, 1),
            nn.Sigmoid()
        )
    def forward(self, image, labels):
        label_embed = self.label_embedding(labels)
        combined_input = torch.cat((image, label_embed),
dim=-1)
        output = self.model(combined_input)
        return output

# Usage Example:
latent_dim = 64
image_dim = 784   # For MNIST (28x28)
num_classes = 10
generator = ConditionalGenerator(latent_dim, num_classes,
image_dim)
discriminator = ConditionalDiscriminator(image_dim,
num_classes)
```

Implementation Notes:

- The generator takes two inputs: a random noise vector and a conditional input (e.g., a class label).
- The discriminator takes two inputs: a data sample (either real or generated) and a conditional input.

- The conditional input is typically embedded using an embedding layer and then concatenated with the other inputs.
- WGAN code will require more substantial modifications to loss functions and discriminators.

Personal Insight: I find conditional GANs to be particularly powerful because they allow you to control the generation process and create data samples with specific characteristics.

Conclusion

DCGAN, WGAN, and Conditional GANs represent significant advancements in the field of GANs, addressing the limitations of the original architecture and expanding its capabilities. By understanding these variants and their underlying principles, you can build more stable, reliable, and controllable GAN models for a wide range of applications. Are you ready to explore the many applications of these models?

8.3 GAN Applications and Challenges - From Image Generation to the Unknown: Exploring the Frontiers and Navigating the Pitfalls

Generative Adversarial Networks (GANs) have captured the imagination of researchers and practitioners alike with their ability to generate new, realistic data samples. Beyond the well-publicized applications in image generation, GANs are finding use in a growing number of diverse fields. However, this powerful technology also presents significant challenges that need to be carefully considered. This section will explore the breadth of GAN applications while also acknowledging the ethical and practical challenges that come with them.

Why Consider GAN Applications and Challenges? It is crucial to understand:

- The wide range of potential applications for GANs beyond image generation.
- The limitations and challenges that need to be addressed to deploy GANs effectively.
- The ethical implications of using GANs and the potential for misuse.

GAN Applications: A World of Possibilities

Let's explore the many areas where GANs are making a significant impact:

- **Image Generation:** Creating new images from scratch, ranging from realistic photographs to artistic creations.
    - *Examples:* Generating new faces, landscapes, and product designs.
- **Image Editing:** Modifying existing images in realistic ways.
    - *Examples:* Changing the hair color, adding glasses, or altering the background of a photograph.
- **Style Transfer:** Transferring the style of one image to another.
    - *Examples:* Turning a photograph into a painting in the style of Van Gogh or Monet.
- **Super-Resolution:** Increasing the resolution of low-resolution images.
    - *Examples:* Generating high-resolution images from blurry or pixelated sources.
- **Image-to-Image Translation:** Transforming images from one domain to another.
    - *Examples:* Converting satellite images to map views or sketches to realistic photos.
- **Data Augmentation:** Generating synthetic data to improve the performance of other models.
    - *Examples:* Generating synthetic images of rare medical conditions to improve the accuracy of diagnostic models.
- **Text-to-Image Synthesis:** Generating images from textual descriptions.
    - *Examples:* Creating images of birds based on textual descriptions of their appearance.
- **Drug Discovery:** Generating new molecules with desired properties.
    - *Examples:* Designing new drugs with high potency and low toxicity.
- **Music Generation:** Creating new music in various styles.
    - *Examples:* Generating new melodies, harmonies, and rhythms.
- **Video Generation:** Creating new videos from scratch.
- **Anonymization Techniques:** Altering sensitive information to protect user information.

Personal Insight: I'm particularly excited about the potential of GANs for drug discovery. The ability to generate new molecules with desired properties could revolutionize the pharmaceutical industry.

Challenges and Limitations: Navigating the Pitfalls of GANs

Despite their potential, GANs also present several challenges that need to be addressed:

- **Training Instability:** GANs can be notoriously difficult to train. The adversarial training process can be unstable, leading to oscillations, mode collapse (where the generator only learns to generate a limited set of data samples), and other issues.
- **Mode Collapse:** The generator learns to produce only a limited set of samples, failing to capture the full diversity of the real data distribution.
- **Evaluation Metrics:** Evaluating the performance of GANs is a challenging problem. There is no single metric that perfectly captures the quality of the generated data. Common metrics include Inception Score (IS) and Fréchet Inception Distance (FID).
- **Computational Resources:** Training GANs can be computationally expensive, requiring significant amounts of memory and processing power.
- **Explainability and Interpretability:** GANs are often considered "black boxes," making it difficult to understand why they generate certain outputs.
- **Bias Amplification:** GANs can amplify biases present in the training data, leading to the generation of biased or discriminatory outputs.

Ethical Considerations: A Responsible Approach

GANs, like any powerful technology, can be used for both good and evil. It's important to be aware of the ethical implications of using GANs and to take steps to prevent their misuse.

- **Deepfakes:** GANs can be used to generate fake images and videos that are difficult to distinguish from real ones. This can be used to spread misinformation, damage reputations, or create propaganda.
- **Bias and Discrimination:** GANs can amplify biases present in the training data, leading to the generation of biased or discriminatory outputs.
- **Privacy Concerns:** GANs can be used to generate synthetic data that reveals sensitive information about individuals or groups.
- **Misinformation:** GANs are used to create fake narratives, generating posts, comments and even personas to spread propaganda.

Personal Insight: It's crucial to consider the ethical implications of your work with GANs and to take steps to mitigate the potential for misuse. As researchers and practitioners, we have a responsibility to ensure that these powerful tools are used for good.

Addressing the Challenges: Research and Best Practices

The GAN research community is actively working to address the challenges and limitations of GANs. Here are some of the areas of active research:

- **Improving Training Stability:** Developing new training techniques and loss functions to stabilize the adversarial training process.
- **Preventing Mode Collapse:** Developing new architectures and training techniques to encourage the generator to explore the full diversity of the data distribution.
- **Developing Better Evaluation Metrics:** Creating new metrics that can more accurately capture the quality and diversity of the generated data.
- **Improving Explainability and Interpretability:** Developing techniques for understanding why GANs generate certain outputs.
- **Mitigating Bias:** Developing techniques for reducing bias in GANs and ensuring that they generate fair and equitable outputs.

Conclusion

GANs are a powerful and rapidly evolving technology with a wide range of applications and significant ethical implications. By understanding the potential of GANs, as well as the challenges and ethical considerations, you can use these tools to create positive change while mitigating the risks. It will be essential to stay up-to-date in the field so that you can continue to make the most informed and responsible decisions as a data scientist. And with that, we have covered an overview of GANs! Onwards!

Chapter 9: Graph Neural Networks (GNNs) - Learning from Relationships: Unlocking the Power of Connected Data

In many real-world scenarios, data is not neatly organized in rows and columns but is instead represented as a graph, consisting of nodes and edges that connect them. Social networks, knowledge graphs, and biological networks are just a few examples of graph-structured data. Graph Neural Networks (GNNs) are a powerful class of neural networks designed to learn from this type of data, enabling you to analyze relationships and make predictions in complex interconnected systems. This chapter is all about looking at data in new ways!

Why Graph Neural Networks Matter: GNNs allow you to:

- Analyze relationships and dependencies between entities.
- Make predictions about nodes, edges, or entire graphs.
- Solve problems that are difficult or impossible to tackle with traditional machine learning methods.
- Find new ways to look at old problems

9.1 Graph Theory Basics for GNNs - Laying the Foundation: Understanding the Language of Relationships

Before diving into the fascinating world of Graph Neural Networks (GNNs), it's essential to establish a firm understanding of the fundamental concepts from graph theory. Just as knowing the grammar and vocabulary of a language is necessary to write compelling stories, grasping the basics of graph theory is crucial for building and interpreting GNNs. This section will equip you with the essential graph theory concepts you'll need to build GNN models, so you can get started!

Why Learn Graph Theory Basics for GNNs? Understanding graph theory allows you to:

- Represent your data in a way that captures relationships and dependencies.

- Choose the right GNN architecture for your specific problem.
- Interpret the results of your GNN models in a meaningful way.

What is a Graph? The Building Block of Relationships

At its core, a graph is a data structure that represents a set of objects and the relationships between them. Think of it as a network of interconnected entities. This network can be used to describe pretty much anything from social relations, to neurons in the brain.

Key Components of a Graph:

- **Nodes (Vertices):** Represent the objects or entities in the graph. They are sometimes called vertices.
- **Edges:** Represent the connections or relationships between the nodes.

Directed vs. Undirected Graphs: Navigating the Flow of Relationships

Graphs can be either directed or undirected, depending on whether the edges have a direction.

- **Directed Graph:** The edges have a direction, indicating a one-way relationship between the nodes. Think of it as one way streets.
- **Undirected Graph:** The edges do not have a direction, indicating a two-way relationship between the nodes. Think of them as roads.

Node Features and Edge Features: Adding Information to the Network

In many real-world applications, nodes and edges have associated attributes or properties that provide additional information about the entities and relationships in the graph. These attributes are represented as *node features* and *edge features*.

Key Concepts:

- **Node Features:** Attributes or properties associated with each node (e.g., age, gender, income for a social network user).
- **Edge Features:** Attributes or properties associated with each edge (e.g., strength of the relationship, type of interaction).

Personal Insight: I often think of node features as the individual characteristics of each person in a social network, while edge features represent the nature and strength of their relationships.

Representing Graphs: Adjacency Matrices and Edge Lists

There are several ways to represent a graph in computer memory. Two of the most common representations are:

- **Adjacency Matrix:** A square matrix where each row and column represents a node in the graph. The element at row i and column j is 1 if there is an edge from node i to node j and 0 otherwise.
- **Edge List:** A list of all the edges in the graph, where each edge is represented as a pair of node indices.

Let's see how to represent a graph using both adjacency matrices and edge lists in PyTorch:

```
import torch
import torch_geometric  #Ensure this is properly installed.

# Example: Representing a graph with an adjacency matrix and
node features
# Graph Example (Undirected):
#        0
#       / \
#      1---2

# Adjacency Matrix
edge_index = torch.tensor([[0, 1, 0, 2, 1, 2], #Edge 0 -> 1,
0 -> 2
                           [1, 0, 2, 0, 2, 1]],
dtype=torch.long) #and 1 ->0, 2 -> 0

# Node Features: Assume each node has 2 features
node_features = torch.tensor([[1.0, 2.0], #Properties of the
node "0"
                              [3.0, 4.0], #Properties of the
node "1"
                              [5.0, 6.0]],
dtype=torch.float32) #Properties of the node "2"

num_nodes = node_features.size(0) #Returns "number of nodes",
size of 0

#Create a graph with torch geometric
from torch_geometric.data import Data
```

```
data = Data(x=node_features, edge_index=edge_index, num_nodes
= num_nodes) #Add number of nodes. This was a parameter that
could automatically load in older versions.

print(f"Graph:\n{data}")
```

Choosing the Right Representation:

- **Adjacency Matrix:** Suitable for dense graphs where most nodes are connected to each other. Easy to perform matrix operations.
- **Edge List:** More memory-efficient for sparse graphs where most nodes are not connected to each other.

Node Degree: Measuring Connectivity

The degree of a node is the number of edges connected to that node. In directed graphs, we distinguish between *in-degree* (number of incoming edges) and *out-degree* (number of outgoing edges).

Building a Graph Data Object in PyTorch Geometric: Simplifying Graph Handling

The torch_geometric library provides a convenient Data class for representing graphs in PyTorch. This class stores the node features, edge list, and other graph-related information in a structured manner.

Personal Insight: Using the Data class from torch_geometric makes it much easier to work with graph data in PyTorch. It handles many of the low-level details for you, allowing you to focus on building your GNN models.

Conclusion

By mastering these basic concepts from graph theory, you'll be well-prepared to explore the fascinating world of Graph Neural Networks (GNNs). You are now able to represent the real world into a data structure that machines can actually process! With this, you will be able to more effectively design, implement, and interpret the results of GNN models. We will look at how to design these models in the next section!

9.2 GNN Architectures: GCNs and GATs - Building Networks for Graph Data: Aggregating Information Across Connections

Now that we have the basics of graph theory under our belt, it's time to explore the architectures that enable us to learn from graph-structured data: Graph Neural Networks (GNNs). Unlike traditional neural networks that operate on grid-like data (e.g., images, text), GNNs are designed to process data that is organized as a graph, consisting of nodes and edges that connect them. Understanding the key architectures can be very helpful when considering new models.

Why Understand GNN Architectures? GNNs have become essential tools for:

- Node Classification: Predicting the labels or attributes of individual nodes in a graph.
- Graph Classification: Predicting the labels or properties of entire graphs.
- Link Prediction: Predicting the existence or strength of connections between nodes.

The Message Passing Paradigm: A Foundation for GNNs

Most GNN architectures follow a message-passing paradigm, which involves iteratively aggregating information from a node's neighbors and updating the node's representation based on this aggregated information. This process allows the network to learn how information flows through the graph and how nodes influence each other.

Key Concepts:

- **Message:** Information that is passed from one node to another along an edge.
- **Aggregation:** Combining the messages from a node's neighbors into a single vector.
- **Update Function:** Updating a node's representation based on the aggregated message.

GCN (Graph Convolutional Network): Averaging the Neighborhood

GCNs (Graph Convolutional Networks) are one of the most fundamental GNN architectures. They aggregate information from a node's neighbors by taking a *weighted average* of their feature vectors. The weights are determined by the graph's adjacency matrix and node degrees.

The GCN Formula:

$h'_i = \sigma(\Sigma_{j \in N(i)} (1/\sqrt{\deg(i)\deg(j)})) * W * h_j)$

Where:

- h'_i is the updated representation of node i.
- $N(i)$ is the set of neighbors of node i.
- $\deg(i)$ is the degree of node i (number of neighbors).
- W is a learnable weight matrix.
- h_j is the representation of neighbor node j.
- σ is an activation function (e.g., ReLU).

Key Intuition: The GCN formula essentially averages the feature vectors of a node's neighbors, weighting each neighbor by the inverse square root of its degree. This helps to normalize the contributions of high-degree nodes, preventing them from dominating the aggregation process.

GAT (Graph Attention Network): Weighing the Importance of Neighbors

GATs (Graph Attention Networks) improve upon GCNs by using an *attention mechanism* to weigh the importance of different neighbors when aggregating information. This allows the network to focus on the most relevant neighbors and to learn more expressive node representations.

The GAT Formula:

$e_{ij} = a(W * h_j \| W * h_i)$

$\alpha_{ij} = \text{softmax}_j(e_{ij})$

$h'_i = \sigma(\Sigma_{j \in N(i)} \alpha_{ij} * W * h_j)$

Where:

- e_{ij} is the attention coefficient between node i and neighbor node j.

- a is a learnable attention function.
- || denotes concatenation.
- α_{ij} is the normalized attention coefficient, obtained by applying the softmax function to the attention scores.
- The other terms are the same as in the GCN formula.

Key Intuition:

- The attention mechanism allows the network to learn which neighbors are most relevant for each node. This is particularly useful when the graph has heterogeneous connections, where some neighbors are more influential than others.
- The attention function a typically consists of a feedforward neural network that takes the concatenated feature vectors of the node and its neighbor as input and outputs a scalar attention score.

Implementing GCNs and GATs with torch_geometric: Simplifying the Process

The torch_geometric library provides convenient classes for implementing GCNs and GATs. Let's see how it works:

```
    import torch
import torch.nn.functional as F
from torch_geometric.nn import GCNConv, GATConv

#Graph Convolutional Network
class GCN(torch.nn.Module):
    def __init__(self, num_node_features, hidden_channels,
num_classes):
        super().__init__()
        torch.manual_seed(12345)
        self.conv1 = GCNConv(num_node_features,
hidden_channels) #Convolution Layer
        self.conv2 = GCNConv(hidden_channels, num_classes)
#Convolution Layer, down to size

    def forward(self, x, edge_index):
        x = self.conv1(x, edge_index) #Propogate graph
        x = x.relu() #Make sure it's relu for non-linearity.
        x = F.dropout(x, p=0.5, training=self.training)
#Implement Dropout
        x = self.conv2(x, edge_index) #Do the next round.
        return x

#Graph Attention Network
```

```
class GAT(torch.nn.Module):
    def __init__(self, num_node_features, hidden_channels,
num_classes, heads):
        super().__init__()
        torch.manual_seed(12345)
        self.gat1 = GATConv(num_node_features,
hidden_channels, heads) #GAT
        self.gat2 = GATConv(hidden_channels * heads,
num_classes, heads) #GAT, notice the number of channels being
modified.

    def forward(self, x, edge_index):
        x = self.gat1(x, edge_index)
        x = x.relu()
        x = F.dropout(x, p=0.5, training=self.training)
#Implement Dropout
        x = self.gat2(x, edge_index)
        return x

#Sample graph data and test
from torch_geometric.data import Data

#Assume graph has been generated. Here is a small sample.
edge_index = torch.tensor([[0, 1, 0, 2, 1, 2],
                           [1, 0, 2, 0, 2, 1]],
dtype=torch.long)

node_features = torch.tensor([[1.0, 2.0],
                              [3.0, 4.0],
                              [5.0, 6.0]],
dtype=torch.float32)

num_nodes = node_features.size(0)

data = Data(x=node_features, edge_index=edge_index, num_nodes
= num_nodes)

# Now test the networks.
#Create the data and test it.
model = GAT(num_node_features = 2, hidden_channels = 4,
num_classes = 2, heads = 2) # Number of heads is important
for GATs
print(model(data.x, data.edge_index))
```

Key Parameters:

- num_node_features: The number of features associated with each node.

- hidden_channels: The number of hidden units in the convolutional layers.
- num_classes: The number of output classes (for node classification).
- heads: The number of attention heads to use in the GATConv layer.

Personal Insight: I've found GCNs to be a good starting point for many graph-based problems. However, if the relationships between nodes are heterogeneous, GATs can often achieve better performance by learning to weigh the importance of different neighbors.

Conclusion

GCNs and GATs are powerful architectures for learning from graph-structured data. By understanding the key concepts of message passing and attention, you can effectively build GNN models that can solve a wide range of problems in various domains. Remember that the graph structure itself informs the network! You can now proceed to explore various uses of this model!

9.3 Applications of GNNs in Various Domains - Connecting the Dots: Unleashing the Power of Relationships

Graph Neural Networks (GNNs) are not just theoretical constructs; they are powerful tools with a wide range of real-world applications. The ability to learn from graph-structured data makes them uniquely suited for tackling problems that are difficult or impossible to solve with traditional machine learning methods. This section will explore the diverse applications of GNNs, showcasing their impact in various domains. This will help you to envision new applications, and how you can utilize the techniques covered thus far.

Why Explore GNN Applications? Understanding the applications of GNNs will inspire you to:

- Identify new problems that can be solved with GNNs.
- Adapt existing GNN architectures to specific application domains.
- Develop novel GNN techniques for addressing unique challenges.

Social Network Analysis: Understanding Human Connections

Social networks are inherently graph-structured, with users representing nodes and connections representing friendships, followerships, or other relationships. GNNs can be used to analyze these networks and gain insights into user behavior, social influence, and community structure.

- **Node Classification:** Predicting user attributes (e.g., age, gender, interests) based on their connections and profile information.
- **Link Prediction:** Recommending new friends or connections to users based on their existing network.
- **Community Detection:** Identifying groups of users with similar interests or connections.

```
#Example code is more advanced, and requires pre-
existing networks and datasets.
print("Social networks can use this to build features on an
existing network, such as making recommendations!")
```

Knowledge Graph Reasoning: Connecting Facts and Inferring New Knowledge

Knowledge graphs are structured representations of facts and relationships between entities. They are used in a wide range of applications, such as question answering, information retrieval, and recommendation systems. GNNs can be used to reason over knowledge graphs and infer new knowledge based on existing facts.

- **Relation Prediction:** Predicting the relationships between entities in a knowledge graph. For example, predicting that "J.K. Rowling" is the "author" of "Harry Potter."
- **Entity Resolution:** Identifying different entities that refer to the same real-world object. For example, determining that "Bill Gates" and "William H. Gates III" refer to the same person.

Recommender Systems: Guiding Users to Relevant Items

Recommender systems are used to suggest items to users based on their past interactions and preferences. GNNs can be used to model the relationships between users and items, allowing for more personalized and accurate recommendations.

- **User-Item Recommendation:** Recommending items to users based on their past interactions and the relationships between items. For example, recommending movies to users based on their viewing history.

- **Cold-Start Recommendation:** Recommending items to new users or items with limited interaction data. GNNs can leverage the relationships between similar users or items to make recommendations even when there is limited data available.

Drug Discovery: Accelerating the Development of New Therapies

Drug discovery is a complex and time-consuming process that involves identifying new molecules with desired properties. GNNs can be used to model the structure and properties of molecules, allowing for more efficient drug discovery.

- **Drug-Target Interaction Prediction:** Predicting which drugs are likely to interact with specific protein targets. This can help to identify promising drug candidates for further development.
- **Molecular Property Prediction:** Predicting the properties of molecules based on their graph structure. For example, predicting the toxicity or efficacy of a drug candidate.

Other Applications: Expanding the Horizon

The applications of GNNs are constantly expanding as researchers discover new ways to leverage their power. Some other notable applications include:

- **Traffic Forecasting:** Predicting traffic flow based on the network of roads and highways.
- **Financial Modeling:** Detecting fraud and predicting market trends based on financial networks.
- **Materials Science:** Designing new materials with desired properties based on their atomic structure.
- **Physics:** Modeling complex processes.

Personal Insight: What I enjoy about GNN is seeing their ability to be used across vastly different fields from physics to chemistry to marketing!

Conclusion

Graph Neural Networks (GNNs) are a versatile and powerful tool for analyzing graph-structured data. From social network analysis to drug discovery, GNNs are finding applications in a wide range of domains, enabling us to understand and solve complex problems in new and innovative ways. Now that you understand their design and various application, you are ready to take these techniques and apply them to your own problems. With this, we move onto how to best train your models!

Chapter 10: Training and Debugging - Mastering the Art of Deep Learning Development

Building and training neural networks is not always a smooth process. It often involves dealing with training instabilities, overfitting, and other challenges. This chapter will equip you with the essential techniques for monitoring your training process, debugging common issues, optimizing your hyperparameters, and saving your models for later use. Think of this chapter as learning to be a skilled mechanic, capable of diagnosing and fixing any problem that arises in your deep learning engine.

Why Training and Debugging Skills Matter: These skills allow you to:

- Train your models more efficiently and effectively.
- Identify and resolve common training issues.
- Improve the performance and generalizability of your models.
- Reproduce your results and share your models with others.

10.1 Monitoring Training: TensorBoard and Logging - Keeping a Close Eye on Your Progress: Your Mission Control for Deep Learning

Training a deep learning model is like piloting a complex spacecraft. You need to constantly monitor various metrics to ensure that everything is running smoothly, identify any potential problems, and make adjustments as needed. Monitoring training with tools like TensorBoard and logging is essential for:

- Understanding how well your model is learning.
- Identifying and resolving training issues early on.
- Optimizing your hyperparameters.
- Reproducing your results and sharing your findings with others.
- Easily see where the points of issues are, such as seeing too much noise or not enough.

Why Monitoring Training Matters: Without proper monitoring, you're flying blind. You might spend hours training a model only to discover that it has overfit the data, failed to converge, or encountered some other unexpected issue. Monitoring ensures that you're on the right track and allows you to make informed decisions throughout the training process.

TensorBoard: Visualizing Your Training Journey

TensorBoard is a powerful visualization toolkit developed by Google for visualizing and understanding your machine learning experiments. It allows you to track various metrics during training, such as:

- **Loss and Accuracy:** Visualize the training and validation loss and accuracy over time.
- **Model Architecture:** View the structure of your neural network.
- **Gradients and Weights:** Monitor the distribution of gradients and weights in your model.
- **Images and Text:** Visualize images and text generated by your model.
- **Custom Scalars and Histograms:** Track any custom metrics that you define.

Key Benefits of TensorBoard:

- **Interactive Visualization:** TensorBoard provides an interactive interface for exploring your training data.
- **Real-Time Monitoring:** You can monitor your training process in real-time, allowing you to quickly identify and respond to any issues.
- **Customizable Dashboards:** You can create custom dashboards to display the metrics that are most important to you.

Let's see how to use TensorBoard in PyTorch:

```python
import torch
import torch.nn as nn
import torch.optim as optim
from torch.utils.tensorboard import SummaryWriter #
TensorBoard

# 1. Create a SummaryWriter
writer = SummaryWriter("runs/experiment_1")  # Specify log
directory. It is important to write to a specific folder so
you can recall previous experiments!

# 2. Define your model, loss function, and optimizer
model = nn.Linear(10, 1) # Or some complex model!
```

```
criterion = nn.MSELoss() #Or your custom Loss
optimizer = optim.Adam(model.parameters(), lr=0.01) #Or
whatever optimizer you're using

# 3. Sample Data. This data was hard coded, but is normally
loaded from a file.
num_examples = 100
x = torch.rand(num_examples, 10)
y = torch.rand(num_examples, 1)

# 4. Training loop
num_epochs = 100
for epoch in range(num_epochs):

    #Zero gradient buffers, propogate and calculate loss.
    y_predicted = model(x)
    loss = criterion(y_predicted, y)

    # Perform the optimization step
    optimizer.zero_grad()
    loss.backward() #Back propogate
    optimizer.step() #Iterate the optimizer

    #Log Values into SummaryWriter. Name value appropriately
    writer.add_scalar("Loss/train", loss, epoch)

# 5. Optional - Look at graph data to see what is happening,
can be memory intensive.
# writer.add_graph(model, inputs) #Add graph to check

# 6. Close after it is finished! IMPORTANT
writer.close()
```

How to Use TensorBoard:

1. **Install TensorBoard:** pip install tensorboard
2. **Run TensorBoard:** Open a terminal and navigate to the directory containing your training script. Then, run the command tensorboard --logdir=runs (or whatever directory you specified for logging).
3. **Access TensorBoard:** Open a web browser and navigate to the address shown in the terminal (usually localhost:6006).

Personal Insight: I always use TensorBoard to monitor my training process. It allows me to quickly identify potential problems, such as overfitting or slow convergence, and to adjust my hyperparameters accordingly.

Logging: Capturing the Details

While TensorBoard provides a powerful visual interface for monitoring your training process, logging allows you to capture more detailed information about your experiments and to store it for later analysis.

Key Information to Log:

- **Hyperparameters:** The values of the hyperparameters that you used for the experiment.
- **Training Metrics:** The loss, accuracy, and other metrics that you tracked during training.
- **Validation Metrics:** The performance of your model on the validation set.
- **Model Checkpoints:** The weights of your model at different points during training.
- **Experiment Configuration:** Any other relevant information about your experiment, such as the dataset used, the code version, and the hardware configuration.

Practical Example:

```
import logging

#1. Define the level of logging we want
logging.basicConfig(level=logging.INFO,
                    format='%(asctime)s - %(levelname)s -
%(message)s',
                    filename='training.log') #Optional - save
log to a file, such as in the cloud.

#Start to add in logs to track what is happening.
logging.info("Training started") #Reported even when quiet
logging.warning("Running out of data.") #Important
information.
logging.error("Division by zero") #Error
```

Personal Insight: You can use Python's built-in logging module, or you can use a more specialized logging library like Weights & Biases for more advanced features.

Conclusion

By mastering the techniques for monitoring your training process with TensorBoard and logging, you can gain valuable insights into how your models are learning and identify any potential problems early on. This will enable you to train more efficient, effective, and reliable deep learning models. This is your mission control for your model! With this information you can properly diagnose issues that occur in the next section!

10.2 Debugging Neural Networks: Common Issues and Solutions - Becoming a Deep Learning Detective

Training neural networks can be a challenging process, and it's not uncommon to encounter issues that prevent your model from learning effectively. Debugging these issues requires a systematic approach, a keen eye for detail, and a solid understanding of the underlying principles. This section is your guide to becoming a deep learning detective, equipping you with the skills to identify, diagnose, and resolve common problems that arise during neural network training. Think of it as learning to use a stethoscope and X-ray machine to diagnose and treat ailments in your deep learning patients.

Why Debugging Skills Matter: The ability to effectively debug neural networks is crucial for:

- Improving model performance.
- Reducing training time.
- Preventing overfitting.
- Gaining a deeper understanding of how your models are working.
- To have your program not tell you errors.

Common Issues and Their Tell-tale Signs

Let's explore some common issues that you might encounter when training neural networks, along with their tell-tale signs and potential solutions:

1. **Vanishing Gradients:**
    - *Tell-tale Signs:* The gradients in the early layers of the network become very small, preventing those layers from learning effectively. The model may converge very slowly or not at all.
    - *Causes:* Use of sigmoid or tanh activation functions, deep networks, poor initialization of weights.

- o *Solutions:*
  - Use ReLU or Leaky ReLU activation functions.
  - Use batch normalization.
  - Use proper weight initialization techniques (e.g., Xavier/Glorot initialization, He initialization).
  - Consider ResNet architectures (using Skip Connections)

2. **Exploding Gradients:**
   - o *Tell-tale Signs:* The gradients become very large, causing the model to become unstable and diverge. You might see NaN values in the loss function.
   - o *Causes:* Large learning rates, deep networks, improper gradient scaling.
   - o *Solutions:*
     - Reduce the learning rate.
     - Use gradient clipping: Limit the magnitude of the gradients to a maximum value.
     - Use batch normalization:
     - Check network design: Is it overly complex? Reduce network size to reduce computation.
   - o Use torch.compile: It can assist with memory issues.

3. **Overfitting:**
   - o *Tell-tale Signs:* The model performs well on the training data but poorly on the validation data. The training accuracy is much higher than the validation accuracy.
   - o *Causes:* Too many parameters, insufficient training data, lack of regularization.
   - o *Solutions:*
     - Increase the size of your dataset: More data can help the model generalize better.
     - Use data augmentation: Create new training samples by applying various transformations to the existing data.
     - Reduce model complexity: Use a smaller architecture with fewer parameters.
     - Use regularization techniques: Apply dropout, batch normalization, or weight decay to prevent overfitting.
     - Early Stopping: Stop when the model stops improving.

4. **Poor Convergence:**

- *Tell-tale Signs:* The model is not converging to a good solution, even after many epochs of training. The loss function may oscillate or plateau at a high value.
- *Causes:* Incorrect learning rate, poor initialization, improper network architechture
- *Solutions:*
  - Adjust the learning rate: Experiment with different learning rates and learning rate schedules.
  - Use a better optimizer: Try Adam or RMSprop instead of SGD.
  - Use batch normalization
  - Implement transfer learning, start from existing models that have been trained.
  - Simplify the network.

5. **Data Issues:**
   - *Tell-tale signs:* The training and validation loss is much worse than expected, and/or does not seem to decrease at all.
   - *Causes:*
     - The labels and data are not properly correlated, or are simply wrong.
     - There is a data leak, so the training set sees the validation set.

Personal Insight: Debugging neural networks is often a process of trial and error. The key is to be systematic, to change only one thing at a time, and to carefully monitor the results. It might take days, weeks, or even months!

Debugging Tools and Techniques

Let's explore the various tools and techniques you can use to diagnose and resolve these common issues:

- **Visualization Tools:**
  - *TensorBoard:* Visualize training metrics (loss, accuracy), model graphs, and parameter distributions.
  - *Weights & Biases:* Another great tool for visualizing and tracking your experiments.
  - *Matplotlib and Seaborn:* Can be used to visualize data, feature maps, and model predictions.
- **Profiling Tools:**
  - *PyTorch Profiler:* Identify performance bottlenecks in your code.

- o *NVIDIA Nsight Systems:* A powerful tool for profiling GPU-accelerated applications.
- **Debugging Techniques:**
  - o *Print Statements:* Use print() statements to inspect the values of tensors and variables during training.
  - o *torch.autograd.set_detect_anomaly(True):* Enable anomaly detection in PyTorch's autograd engine to catch errors related to gradient computations.
  - o *Unit Tests:* Write unit tests to verify the correctness of individual components of your model.

Practical Notes:

- Use the tools available! You can save time and effort!
- Learn how to use these tools from their respective documentations.

Code Examples

```
    #Useful Code snippets!
#Gradient Clipping
torch.nn.utils.clip_grad_norm_(model.parameters(),
max_norm=1) #Set to 1

#Anamoly Detection
torch.autograd.set_detect_anomaly(True) #Find the source of
errors.

#Setting Device for CUDA
if torch.cuda.is_available():
    device = torch.device("cuda")
    print("CUDA is available. Using GPU.")
else:
    device = torch.device("cpu")
    print("CUDA is not available. Using CPU.")

#Moving to CUDA
model = model.to(device)
inputs = inputs.to(device) #Or tensors to whatever data you
may need

#Free CUDA Memory
del inputs, outputs, loss #clear values
torch.cuda.empty_cache() #clear the GPU
```

Personal Insight: I rely heavily on TensorBoard for monitoring my training progress and identifying potential problems. The ability to visualize the loss curves and other metrics in real-time is invaluable for debugging. I also use the print statements when it doesn't fit my needs.

The Zen of Debugging: A Mindset for Success

- **Be Patient:** Debugging can be a time-consuming process. Don't get discouraged if you don't find the solution immediately.
- **Be Systematic:** Change only one thing at a time and carefully monitor the results.
- **Be Curious:** Explore the data, the model, and the training process to gain a deeper understanding of what's going on.
- **Ask for Help:** Don't be afraid to ask for help from the PyTorch community. There are many experienced developers who are willing to share their knowledge and expertise.

Conclusion

Debugging neural networks is a challenging but rewarding skill. By understanding the common issues, using the right tools and techniques, and adopting a patient and systematic approach, you can effectively diagnose and resolve problems, leading to more accurate, robust, and efficient deep learning models. With these principles, you can approach a problem with comfort knowing you have the right methodology!

10.3 Hyperparameter Optimization: Strategies and Tools - Finding the Optimal Configuration: The Art of Fine-Tuning

The performance of a neural network is heavily dependent on the choice of hyperparameters. Hyperparameters are the settings that control the learning process itself, such as the learning rate, batch size, regularization strength, and network architecture. Finding the optimal set of hyperparameters is crucial for maximizing the performance of your model, but it can also be a time-consuming and challenging task. Think of this as being a conductor: it is still you who will be making the final decisions, but understanding what options are available for the instruments gives you the ability to arrange and modify the melody as you see fit.

Why Hyperparameter Optimization Matters: A well-tuned set of hyperparameters can lead to:

- Faster convergence.
- Improved accuracy.
- Better generalization performance.
- More robust models.

The Challenge of Hyperparameter Optimization: A Complex Search Space

The search space for hyperparameters can be vast and complex. The optimal values for different hyperparameters often depend on each other, making it difficult to find the best configuration. Moreover, evaluating each hyperparameter configuration requires training a model, which can be computationally expensive.

Hyperparameter Optimization Strategies: A Toolkit for Finding the Best Settings

Let's explore some of the most common and effective strategies for hyperparameter optimization:

- **Manual Tuning:** This involves experimenting with different hyperparameter values manually, based on your intuition and experience. This approach can be useful for gaining a better understanding of how different hyperparameters affect the model's performance, but it can be time-consuming and inefficient.

  Personal Insight: I often start with manual tuning to get a feel for the search space and identify the most important hyperparameters to focus on.

- **Grid Search:** This involves systematically trying all possible combinations of hyperparameter values within a predefined range. This approach is guaranteed to find the optimal configuration (within the specified range), but it can be computationally expensive, especially when dealing with a large number of hyperparameters or a large search space.
- **Random Search:** This involves randomly sampling hyperparameter values from a predefined distribution. This approach is often more

efficient than grid search, especially when some hyperparameters are more important than others.

- **Bayesian Optimization:** This is a more advanced technique that uses a probabilistic model to guide the search for the optimal hyperparameters. It balances exploration (trying new hyperparameter values) and exploitation (focusing on hyperparameter values that have performed well in the past). This approach can be more efficient than grid search and random search, especially when the evaluation of each hyperparameter configuration is expensive. Bayesian methods try to model results based on previous trials so that future runs do not waste compute or time.

Tools for Hyperparameter Optimization: Automating the Process

Several tools can help you automate the hyperparameter optimization process. Here are a few popular options:

- **scikit-optimize (skopt):** A Python library that provides implementations of Bayesian optimization and other optimization algorithms.
- **Optuna:** A flexible and scalable hyperparameter optimization framework.
- **Weights & Biases (W&B):** A platform for tracking and visualizing machine learning experiments, with built-in support for hyperparameter optimization.

Using scikit-optimize for Bayesian Optimization:

```
import torch
import torch.optim as optim
from skopt import BayesSearchCV
from sklearn.model_selection import train_test_split
from sklearn.linear_model import SGDClassifier

#This only provides an outline since most models have custom
configurations.
#In this case, the underlying model uses sklearn to build and
train
#We will select some sample parameters and apply to them.

# 1. Set the parameters to search
param_grid = {
    'alpha': (1e-6, 1e-4, 'log-uniform'),
    'l1_ratio': (0, 1),
    'eta0': (1e-5, 1e-1, 'log-uniform'),
```

```
}

# 2. Set all the configurations of the model. In this case,
fit intercept, iterations and random state.
bs = BayesSearchCV(SGDClassifier(loss='log_loss',
fit_intercept=True, max_iter=5, tol=None, random_state=0),
                search_spaces=param_grid, #Sets up how
what are the various combinations that can be run.
                cv=3, #Cross validations, sets up training
and tests.
                n_iter=50, #Number of iterations to search
for an approach
                verbose=0,
                random_state=0,
                n_jobs=3)
```

Personal Insight: I've found Bayesian optimization to be a very effective technique for hyperparameter tuning, especially when I have a limited budget for training models. It allows me to explore the search space more efficiently and find better configurations with fewer trials.

Best Practices for Hyperparameter Optimization: A Strategic Approach

- **Define a Clear Objective:** Clearly define the metric that you want to optimize (e.g., validation accuracy, F1-score).
- **Choose a Suitable Search Space:** Define a realistic range of values for each hyperparameter.
- **Use a Validation Set:** Evaluate the performance of each hyperparameter configuration on a validation set to prevent overfitting.
- **Start with a Coarse Search:** First, perform a coarse search to identify the most promising regions of the search space. Then, perform a finer search within those regions.
- **Track Your Experiments:** Use a tool like Weights & Biases to track your experiments, compare different hyperparameter configurations, and visualize your results.

Conclusion

Hyperparameter optimization is an essential step in building high-performance neural networks. By understanding the different optimization strategies and tools available, you can effectively fine-tune your models and achieve optimal performance. By doing so, you will be able to achieve new peaks in the models you design. Now, onward, to discuss methods to preserve your model and it's learnings!

10.4 Checkpointing and Model Saving - Preserving Your Progress: Ensuring Your Model's Longevity

After the arduous process of training a neural network, it's essential to save your progress. Checkpointing and model saving are fundamental practices that allow you to preserve your trained models, resume training from a specific point, and deploy your models for inference. Think of this section as building a secure vault for your hard-earned deep learning treasures. This ensures that you will not need to retrain the whole thing again, and that it can be retrieved whenever needed.

Why Checkpointing and Model Saving Matters: These techniques allow you to:

- Resume training from a specific point if your training process is interrupted.
- Load and use your trained models for inference.
- Reproduce your results and share your models with others.
- Deploy Models with confidence.

Checkpointing: Saving Progress Mid-Training

Checkpointing involves saving the model's parameters and other training-related information at regular intervals during training. This allows you to resume training from a specific point if your training process is interrupted (e.g., due to a power outage or a system crash).

What to Include in a Checkpoint:

- **Model's state_dict():** A dictionary containing the model's learnable parameters (weights and biases).
- **Optimizer's state_dict():** A dictionary containing the optimizer's state (e.g., learning rate, momentum).
- **Epoch Number:** The current epoch number.
- **Loss Value:** The loss value at the time of saving the checkpoint.
- **Any Other Relevant Information:** Any other information that is needed to resume training from the checkpoint.

Model Saving: Preserving the Final Result

Model saving involves saving the final trained model to a file. This allows you to load and use the model for inference without having to retrain it from scratch.

Different Ways to Save a Model:

- **Saving the Entire Model:** Saves the entire model architecture and its parameters. This is the most convenient way to save a model, but it can be less flexible if you want to modify the model architecture later.
- **Saving Only the Model's state_dict():** Saves only the model's parameters. This is more flexible, as it allows you to load the parameters into a different model architecture, but it requires you to define the model architecture separately.

Best Practices

1. Pick a descriptive file name, for both saving and restoring the model.
2. Check the loaded parameters against expected performance to make sure it was properly loaded.

Code Example:

```
import torch

# Assuming you have model, optimizer, loss, and epoch #
defined

PATH = "my_model.pth" #Good to indicate what the path
actually is.

#Example saving
torch.save({'epoch': epoch,
          'model_state_dict': model.state_dict(),
          'optimizer_state_dict': optimizer.state_dict(),
          'loss': loss,
          }, PATH)

#Example loading it back in
model = TheModelClass(*args, **kwargs)
optimizer = TheOptimizerClass(*args, **kwargs)

checkpoint = torch.load(PATH) #Can load based on CUDA here
model.load_state_dict(checkpoint['model_state_dict'])
```

```
optimizer.load_state_dict(checkpoint['optimizer_state_dict'])
epoch = checkpoint['epoch']
loss = checkpoint['loss']

model.eval() #Or model.train() # depending on what you want.

#Model is ready to resume.
```

Personal Insight: I always save the optimizer's state along with the model's parameters. This allows me to resume training from a checkpoint without having to reset the optimizer's learning rate and other parameters.

Loading the Model on Different Devices: Handling GPU vs. CPU

When loading a model that was trained on a GPU, you may need to load it onto a different device (e.g., a CPU) or a different GPU. PyTorch provides several ways to handle this:

- **Loading onto the CPU:** Use the map_location argument in torch.load() to map the tensors to the CPU.

```
    #Example of loading on the CPU
device = torch.device('cpu')
model = TheModelClass(*args, **kwargs)
model.load_state_dict(torch.load(PATH, map_location=device))
model.to(device) #Set the device to CPU for processing.
```

- **Loading onto a Different GPU:** Use the torch.cuda.set_device() function to set the current GPU device before loading the model.

Practical Considerations:

- **Version Compatibility:** Make sure that the PyTorch version used to load the model is compatible with the version used to save it.
- **File Size:** Saving the entire model can result in large files, especially for complex architectures. Consider saving only the model's state_dict() to reduce the file size.
- **Security:** Be careful when loading models from untrusted sources, as they may contain malicious code.

Conclusion

Checkpointing and model saving are essential practices for any deep learning project. By mastering these techniques, you can ensure that your hard-earned progress is preserved, that you can easily reproduce your results, and that you can deploy your models with confidence.

Part III: Deployment, Optimization, and Advanced Techniques

Chapter 11: Model Deployment - Bringing Your Deep Learning Creations to the Real World

You've trained a fantastic model, achieving impressive accuracy on your validation set. Now, it's time to unleash it upon the real world! Model deployment involves taking your trained model and making it available for use in production environments, where it can make predictions on new, unseen data. This chapter is about giving your models their wings and helping them soar in real-world applications.

Why Model Deployment Matters: A model that's not deployed is a model that's not making an impact. Deployment is the crucial step that transforms your research project into a valuable tool for solving real-world problems.

11.1 Saving and Loading PyTorch Models - The Foundation for Deployment: Preserving Your Hard Work

In the grand scheme of deep learning, training a model is only half the battle. Once you've spent hours (or even days!) training a model to achieve satisfactory performance, you'll want to save it so you can reuse it later for inference, deployment, or further training. Saving and loading PyTorch models is a fundamental skill for any deep learning practitioner. It ensures that your hard work isn't lost and allows you to easily share and deploy your models.

Why Saving and Loading Models Matters: This process allows you to:

- Reuse trained models for inference without retraining.
- Share your models with others.
- Resume training from a specific checkpoint.
- Deploy your models to production environments.

Serialization and Deserialization: Transforming Models into Files

Saving and loading PyTorch models involves a process called serialization and deserialization. Serialization is the process of converting a PyTorch model (which is essentially a Python object) into a stream of bytes that can be stored in a file. Deserialization is the reverse process of converting the byte stream back into a PyTorch model.

Saving Model Parameters: The Recommended Approach

The recommended way to save PyTorch models is to save the model's *state dictionary*. The state dictionary contains all the learnable parameters of the model (i.e., the weights and biases of the layers).

Advantages of Saving State Dictionaries:

- **Lightweight and Efficient:** State dictionaries are typically smaller than saving the entire model, as they only store the parameters.
- **Flexibility:** State dictionaries can be loaded into models with different architectures, as long as the layer names and dimensions match.
- **Stability:** State dictionaries are less prone to compatibility issues between different PyTorch versions.

```python
import torch
import torch.nn as nn

# 1. Define a Model (example)
class SimpleNet(nn.Module):
    def __init__(self, input_size, hidden_size, output_size):
        super(SimpleNet, self).__init__()
        self.fc1 = nn.Linear(input_size, hidden_size)
        self.relu = nn.ReLU()
        self.fc2 = nn.Linear(hidden_size, output_size)

    def forward(self, x):
        x = self.fc1(x)
        x = self.relu(x)
        x = self.fc2(x)
        return x

# 2. Instantiate the Model and train it
input_size = 10
hidden_size = 5
output_size = 1
model = SimpleNet(input_size, hidden_size, output_size)

#Train the Model before the Save.

# 3. Save the Model's State Dictionary
FILE_PATH = 'model.pth'
```

```
torch.save(model.state_dict(), FILE_PATH) # Saves the weights
and biases, but not the structure!
print(f"State dictionary saved to {FILE_PATH}")
```

Important Notes:

- We use torch.save() to save the state dictionary to a file with the .pth extension (which is a common convention for PyTorch models).
- The FILE_PATH variable specifies the path to the file where the state dictionary will be saved.
- The example does not train the model. You must train the model first before saving it to capture the trained weights.

Loading a Saved State Dictionary: Restoring Your Model

To load a saved state dictionary, you need to follow these steps:

1. Create an instance of the model with the same architecture as the model that was used to generate the state dictionary.
2. Load the state dictionary from the file using torch.load().
3. Load the state dictionary into the model using model.load_state_dict().

```
import torch
import torch.nn as nn

# 1. Define the Same Model (Same Architecture)
class SimpleNet(nn.Module):
    def __init__(self, input_size, hidden_size, output_size):
        super(SimpleNet, self).__init__()
        self.fc1 = nn.Linear(input_size, hidden_size)
        self.relu = nn.ReLU()
        self.fc2 = nn.Linear(hidden_size, output_size)

    def forward(self, x):
        x = self.fc1(x)
        x = self.relu(x)
        x = self.fc2(x)
        return x

# 2. Instantiate the Model (same architecture as above)
input_size = 10
hidden_size = 5
output_size = 1
loaded_model = SimpleNet(input_size, hidden_size,
output_size)
```

```
# 3. Load the State Dictionary
FILE_PATH = 'model.pth'
loaded_model.load_state_dict(torch.load(FILE_PATH)) # Loads
the weights and biases into the model from the file.
loaded_model.eval() #Sets model to eval phase.

print(f"Loaded the weights, and set the model up for
evaluation.")
```

Best Practice: ALWAYS make sure the model structure matches!

Important Notes:

- The model architecture must be the same as the model that was used to generate the state dictionary. Otherwise, the load_state_dict() method will raise an error.
- We call model.eval() after loading the state dictionary to set the model to evaluation mode. This is important because some layers, such as dropout and batch normalization, behave differently during training and evaluation.

Saving and Loading the Entire Model: A Less Flexible Approach

While saving the state dictionary is generally recommended, you can also save the entire model using torch.save(model, FILE_PATH). This approach saves both the model's architecture and its parameters.

Disadvantages of Saving the Entire Model:

- **Larger File Size:** Saving the entire model typically results in a larger file size than saving the state dictionary.
- **Less Flexibility:** The loaded model must have the exact same architecture and dependencies as the model that was saved.
- **Compatibility Issues:** Loading an entire model can be more prone to compatibility issues between different PyTorch versions.

Saving Additional Information: Creating Checkpoints

In addition to saving the model's parameters, you can also save other information, such as the optimizer's state, the learning rate, and the current epoch number. This allows you to create checkpoints that can be used to resume training from a specific point.

```python
import torch
import torch.nn as nn
import torch.optim as optim

# Example: Saving and loading a checkpoint

# Training loop for checkpoint
def save_checkpoint():
    FILE_PATH = 'checkpoint.pth'
    checkpoint = {
        'epoch': epoch,
        'model_state': model.state_dict(),
        'optimizer_state': optimizer.state_dict(),
        'loss': loss,
    }
    torch.save(checkpoint, FILE_PATH)

def load_checkpoint():
  FILE_PATH = 'checkpoint.pth'
  checkpoint = torch.load(FILE_PATH) #Loads weights into
checkpoint
  model.load_state_dict(checkpoint['model_state']) #Loads
weights
  optimizer.load_state_dict(checkpoint['optimizer_state'])
#Loads optimizer too.
  epoch = checkpoint['epoch'] #Loads the epoch.
  loss = checkpoint['loss'] #Can load the loss.

  return epoch, loss
```

Loading on Different Devices: GPU vs. CPU

When loading a model that was trained on a GPU, you may need to specify the map_location argument to torch.load() if you're loading the model on a CPU.

```python
    #Code
FILE_PATH = 'model.pth'
device = torch.device('cuda' if torch.cuda.is_available()
else 'cpu')
model = SimpleNet(input_size, hidden_size, output_size) #Set
to Model
model.load_state_dict(torch.load(FILE_PATH,
map_location=device)) #Will automatically change it to CUDA
or CPU

#If loading on CPU after training on GPU, you'll need this to
"map" the CUDA to the CPU.
#torch.load(PATH, map_location=torch.device('cpu'))
```

Important Notes:

- The map_location argument specifies the device (CPU or GPU) where the model should be loaded.
- If you're loading the model on a GPU, you don't need to specify map_location.

Personal Insight: Saving and loading models is a crucial skill for any deep learning practitioner. I always make sure to save my models regularly during training, especially when training on large datasets. This allows me to resume training from a specific checkpoint if something goes wrong.

Conclusion

Saving and loading PyTorch models is a fundamental skill that enables you to reuse, share, and deploy your trained models. By understanding the different approaches and best practices, you can ensure that your hard work is preserved and easily accessible. By taking the time to follow best practices, you have set up a foundation for further development in deployment! Time to look at TorchScript!

11.2 TorchScript: Deployment-Ready Models - Compiling for Performance and Portability: Bridging the Gap Between Research and Production

While PyTorch is incredibly flexible and powerful for research and development, deploying PyTorch models to production environments can present challenges. TorchScript is PyTorch's solution to these challenges. It's a way to *compile* your PyTorch models into a static graph representation, enabling them to run efficiently in environments where Python may not be available or where you need to optimize for performance. Think of TorchScript as baking a cake – you take the raw ingredients (your PyTorch code) and transform them into a pre-compiled, readily consumable product (a TorchScript module).

Why TorchScript Matters: TorchScript allows you to:

- **Improve Performance:** TorchScript models can be optimized for speed and memory usage.

- **Achieve Portability:** TorchScript models can be run in a variety of environments, including C++, Java, and mobile devices, without requiring a Python interpreter.
- **Enhance Stability:** TorchScript models are less prone to runtime errors due to their static graph representation.
- **Enable Tooling:** TorchScript unlocks powerful tooling for optimization, quantization, and model analysis.

Tracing vs. Scripting: Two Paths to TorchScript

There are two main ways to convert a PyTorch model to TorchScript:

- **Tracing:** This approach involves running your model with sample inputs and recording the operations that are performed. TorchScript then creates a graph representation of these operations. This is a relatively simple approach, but it can be limited if your model contains control flow (e.g., if statements or loops) that depends on the input data.
- **Scripting:** This approach involves directly annotating your PyTorch code with special decorators that tell TorchScript how to compile the model. This is more flexible than tracing and can handle control flow, but it requires more effort to implement.

Tracing: A Quick and Easy Start

Tracing is a good option for simple models that don't have complex control flow.

```python
import torch
import torch.nn as nn

# 1. Define a Model (example)
class SimpleNet(nn.Module):
    def __init__(self, input_size, hidden_size, output_size):
        super(SimpleNet, self).__init__()
        self.fc1 = nn.Linear(input_size, hidden_size)
        self.relu = nn.ReLU()
        self.fc2 = nn.Linear(hidden_size, output_size)

    def forward(self, x):
        x = self.fc1(x)
        x = self.relu(x)
        x = self.fc2(x)
        return x
```

```
# 2. Instantiate the Model
input_size = 10
hidden_size = 5
output_size = 1
model = SimpleNet(input_size, hidden_size, output_size)

# 3. Create Sample Input
example = torch.rand(1, input_size)  # Example of input for
tracing.

# 4. Trace the Model
traced_script_module = torch.jit.trace(model, example)

# 5. Save the TorchScript Module
traced_script_module.save("traced_model.pt")

print("Traced model saved as traced_model.pt")
```

Understanding the Code:

- We use torch.jit.trace() to trace the model, providing the model and an example input.
- The example input is used to run the model and record the operations that are performed.
- The traced_script_module object represents the compiled TorchScript module.
- We use traced_script_module.save() to save the TorchScript module to a file with the .pt extension.

Scripting: Handling Control Flow

Scripting provides more control over the compilation process and can handle models with complex control flow.

```
import torch
import torch.nn as nn

# 1. Define a Model (example)
class ConditionalNet(nn.Module):
    def __init__(self, input_size, hidden_size, output_size):
        super(ConditionalNet, self).__init__()
        self.fc1 = nn.Linear(input_size, hidden_size)
        self.relu = nn.ReLU()
        self.fc2 = nn.Linear(hidden_size, output_size)
```

```
    @torch.jit.script_method  # Add script_method for
conditional flow
    def forward(self, x, condition: bool): #Annotate the
function with the bool
        x = self.fc1(x)
        x = self.relu(x)
        if condition:
            x = x * 2 #Custom actions when condition is met
        x = self.fc2(x)
        return x

# 2. Instantiate the Model
input_size = 10
hidden_size = 5
output_size = 1
model = ConditionalNet(input_size, hidden_size, output_size)

# 3. Script the Model
scripted_module = torch.jit.script(model)

# 4. Save the TorchScript Module
scripted_module.save("scripted_model.pt") #Name and save.

print("Scripted model saved as scripted_model.pt")
```

Understanding the Code:

- We use the @torch.jit.script decorator to tell TorchScript to compile the model.
- The @torch.jit.script_method decorator is needed when the flow is dependent on one of the inputs. Also, you need to specify which input is the type, such as condition : bool.

Loading a TorchScript Module: Deploying Your Model

To load a TorchScript module, you can use torch.jit.load().

```
    import torch

# Load the TorchScript Module
loaded_model = torch.jit.load("scripted_model.pt") #Can load
script or traces.

# Set the Model to Evaluation Mode
loaded_model.eval() #Always load on Eval

# Create Sample Input for testing
```

```
sample_input = torch.rand(1, 10)

# Run Inference and see its results.
sample_condition = torch.tensor([True])
with torch.no_grad():
    prediction = loaded_model(sample_input, sample_condition)

print(f"Predictions = {prediction}")
```

Practical Notes:

- Loading can occur in C++
- It can run without Torch installed as well.

Personal Insight: TorchScript has been a game-changer for deploying PyTorch models. It allows me to easily optimize my models for performance and deploy them to a wide range of environments. I am ready to get off the Python runtime system!

Conclusion

TorchScript is a powerful tool for bridging the gap between research and production in PyTorch. By compiling your models to TorchScript, you can improve their performance, portability, and stability, making them ready for deployment in a wide range of environments. With this, you have the key skills required for the next step! Let's talk quantization!

11.3 ONNX Export: Cross-Framework Compatibility - Sharing Your Models with the World: Breaking Down the Silos

While PyTorch is a fantastic framework for building and training deep learning models, the reality is that different deployment environments and hardware platforms may have better support for other frameworks. This is where ONNX (Open Neural Network Exchange) comes to the rescue. ONNX is an open standard for representing machine learning models, allowing you to easily convert models from one framework to another. Think of ONNX as a universal translator for machine learning models, enabling them to be shared and deployed across different platforms and frameworks without requiring code modifications.

Why ONNX Export Matters: ONNX allows you to:

- **Achieve Cross-Framework Compatibility:** Export your PyTorch models to ONNX format and run them in other frameworks like TensorFlow, CoreML, or ONNX Runtime.
- **Leverage Hardware Acceleration:** Utilize hardware acceleration libraries optimized for ONNX Runtime on different platforms.
- **Simplify Deployment:** Deploy your models to a wider range of environments without needing to rewrite them in different frameworks.
- **Enable Interoperability:** Integrate your PyTorch models with other tools and systems that support ONNX.

Understanding ONNX: A Standardized Representation

ONNX defines a standardized set of operators and a common file format for representing neural network models. This allows different frameworks to import and export models in a consistent manner, ensuring interoperability.

Exporting PyTorch Models to ONNX: A Step-by-Step Guide

Exporting a PyTorch model to ONNX is relatively straightforward using the torch.onnx.export() function.

```python
import torch
import torch.nn as nn

# 1. Define a Model (example)
class SimpleNet(nn.Module):
    def __init__(self, input_size, hidden_size, output_size):
        super(SimpleNet, self).__init__()
        self.fc1 = nn.Linear(input_size, hidden_size)
        self.relu = nn.ReLU()
        self.fc2 = nn.Linear(hidden_size, output_size)

    def forward(self, x):
        x = self.fc1(x)
        x = self.relu(x)
        x = self.fc2(x)
        return x

# 2. Instantiate the Model
input_size = 10
hidden_size = 5
output_size = 1
model = SimpleNet(input_size, hidden_size, output_size)
```

```
# 3. Create Sample Input
example = torch.randn(1, input_size)

# 4. Export the Model to ONNX

FILE_PATH = "simplenet.onnx" #Name the output as .onnx
torch.onnx.export(model,                        # model being
run
                  example,                      # model input
(or a tuple for multiple inputs)
                  FILE_PATH,                           # where
to save the model (can be a file or file-like object)
                  export_params=True,           # store the
trained parameter weights inside the model file
                  opset_version=10,                  # the ONNX
version to use
                  do_constant_folding=True,   # whether to
execute constant folding for optimization
                  input_names = ['input'],     # the
model's input names
                  output_names = ['output'])  # the
model's output names

print(f"Model exported to ONNX format at {FILE_PATH}")
```

Understanding the Parameters:

- model: The PyTorch model to be exported.
- args: The model input (or a tuple for multiple inputs). This is used to trace the model's execution and determine the ONNX graph.
- f: The file path where the ONNX model will be saved.
- export_params: Whether to store the trained parameter weights inside the ONNX model file. Set to True for most use cases.
- opset_version: The ONNX version to use. A higher version may support more operators but may not be compatible with all frameworks.
- do_constant_folding: Whether to perform constant folding optimization, which can improve the model's performance.
- input_names: A list of names for the model's inputs.
- output_names: A list of names for the model's outputs.

Verifying the ONNX Export: Ensuring Correctness

After exporting the model to ONNX format, it's important to verify that the export was successful and that the ONNX model produces the same results as the original PyTorch model.

```python
import onnx
import onnxruntime
import numpy as np

# 1. Load the ONNX Model
onnx_model = onnx.load("simplenet.onnx")
onnx.checker.check_model(onnx_model) #Check model to see if
it loaded right

# 2. Create an ONNX Runtime Inference Session
ort_session = onnxruntime.InferenceSession("simplenet.onnx")

# 3. Run Inference with ONNX Runtime
def to_numpy(tensor):
    return tensor.detach().cpu().numpy() if
tensor.requires_grad else tensor.cpu().numpy()

# Sample input
ort_inputs = {ort_session.get_inputs()[0].name:
to_numpy(example)} #Set as numpy

# Run Inference
ort_outs = ort_session.run(None, ort_inputs) #Get results as
array
ort_outs = ort_outs[0]

print(f"Sample array = {ort_outs}")
```

Tips and Considerations:

- Test as many scenarios as possible, and compare with the output from Torch.
- Remember to ensure your input tensors to be Numpy objects
- Test to see if the results are similar
- Run the onnx simplifier as a step as well.

Personal Insight: Exporting to ONNX allows me to work around limitations in Pytorch, whether by using a tool that has a better integration with onnx, or to allow deployment on systems without PyTorch!

Conclusion

ONNX export is a valuable tool for achieving cross-framework compatibility and deploying your PyTorch models to a wider range of environments. By understanding the ONNX format and how to export your models, you can break down the silos between different frameworks and leverage the best tools for your specific deployment needs. You are now ready to share your models across the world!

11.4 Deployment Platforms: Cloud and Edge - Where Your Models Take Flight: From the Lab to the Real World

After training, optimizing, and packaging your PyTorch model, the final step is deployment. This is where your model takes flight and starts solving real-world problems. Choosing the right deployment platform is crucial for ensuring that your model is accessible, scalable, and performs reliably in the intended environment. The two primary deployment paradigms are Cloud and Edge.

Why Choosing the Right Platform Matters: The deployment platform will directly affect:

- **Scalability:** How well your model can handle increasing traffic or data volume.
- **Latency:** The time it takes for your model to generate a prediction.
- **Cost:** The expenses associated with running your model.
- **Security and Privacy:** How well your model and data are protected.
- **Accessibility:** How easy it is for users to access your model.

Cloud Deployment: Harnessing the Power of the Internet

Cloud deployment involves hosting your model on a remote server or a cloud platform like AWS, Google Cloud, or Azure. This allows you to leverage the vast resources of the cloud to scale your model and make it accessible to users from anywhere in the world.

Advantages of Cloud Deployment:

- **Scalability:** Cloud platforms can automatically scale your model to handle fluctuating traffic demands.
- **Accessibility:** Your model is accessible to users from anywhere with an internet connection.

- **Cost-Effectiveness:** Cloud platforms offer pay-as-you-go pricing models, allowing you to pay only for the resources you use.
- **Managed Infrastructure:** Cloud providers handle the underlying infrastructure, freeing you from managing servers and networks.

Common Cloud Deployment Options:

- **AWS (Amazon Web Services):**
  - *SageMaker:* A fully managed machine learning service that provides tools for building, training, and deploying machine learning models.
  - *EC2:* Virtual servers that you can use to host your model and deploy it using a web framework like Flask or Django.
  - *Lambda:* Serverless compute service that allows you to run your model without managing servers.
- **Google Cloud Platform (GCP):**
  - *Vertex AI:* A unified platform for machine learning that provides tools for building, training, and deploying machine learning models.
  - *Compute Engine:* Virtual machines that you can use to host your model and deploy it using a web framework.
  - *Cloud Functions:* Serverless compute service similar to AWS Lambda.
- **Azure (Microsoft Azure):**
  - *Azure Machine Learning:* A cloud-based platform for building, training, and deploying machine learning models.
  - *Virtual Machines:* Virtual machines that you can use to host your model and deploy it using a web framework.
  - *Azure Functions:* Serverless compute service similar to AWS Lambda and Google Cloud Functions.

Simplified Code for Basic Cloud Deployment Using Flask and TorchServe (Example - Assumes you've TorchScripted your model to model.pt from a prior step):

This approach has some limitations, however it's much easier and faster to deploy this way.

```
from flask import Flask, request, jsonify
import torch

#Setup web application
app = Flask(__name__)
```

```python
#Load in the model - needs to be a torchscripted model!
FILE_PATH = 'model.pt' #Name of the model
model = torch.jit.load(FILE_PATH) #Loads the model and
weights

#Setup device for calculation
model.eval()
device = torch.device('cuda' if torch.cuda.is_available()
else 'cpu') #Uses GPU
model.to(device)

#Create the route - called from HTTP
@app.route('/predict', methods=['POST'])
def predict():
    if request.method == 'POST': #Only for POST calls
        try:
            data = request.get_json() #Get data from the
request - needs to be a JSON value
            input_data = data['data'] #Get data key
            input_tensor = torch.tensor(input_data,
dtype=torch.float32).unsqueeze(0).to(device) #Convert to
tensors

            with torch.no_grad():
                prediction = model(input_tensor) #Feed into
the model

            output = prediction.cpu().numpy().tolist()
#Extract output to view.
            return jsonify({'prediction': output})

        except Exception as e:
            return jsonify({'error': str(e)})
    else:
        return "Only POST requests allowed."

if __name__ == '__main__':
    app.run(debug=True)
```

TorchServe Approach:

TorchServe is a more optimized framework for deployment on AWS. It is more complex to set up initially but ultimately pays off if you're using many different models.

1. **Install TorchServe and TorchModelArchiver:**

```
pip install torchserve torch-model-archiver
```

2. **Create a Model Handler:** This is a Python class that defines how your model will be loaded, preprocessed, and postprocessed.
3. **Create a Configuration File (optional):** This file allows you to customize the behavior of TorchServe.
4. **Archive the Model:** Use the torch-model-archiver tool to create a model archive file (.mar).

```
torch-model-archiver --model-name my_model \
            --version 1.0 \
            --model-file model.py \
            --handler handler.py \
            --serialized-file model.pth \
            --export-path model_store
```

5. **Start TorchServe:**

```
torchserve --model-store model_store --models
my_model=my_model.mar --host 0.0.0.0 --port 8080
```

6. **Make Predictions:** Send requests to your TorchServe endpoint to get predictions.

Personal Insight: Flask is a good start as it is simpler. TorchServe takes the lead with features such as optimized scaling. Choose based on your requirements for throughput.

Edge Deployment: Bringing Intelligence Closer to the Data

Edge deployment involves running your model on devices that are located closer to the data source, such as mobile phones, IoT devices, or edge servers. This can significantly reduce latency and improve privacy, as the data doesn't need to be transmitted to the cloud for processing.

Advantages of Edge Deployment:

- **Low Latency:** Edge deployment reduces the latency associated with sending data to the cloud and receiving predictions.
- **Privacy:** Data is processed locally on the device, reducing the risk of sensitive data being exposed to the cloud.

- **Offline Functionality:** Edge deployment allows your model to function even when there is no internet connection.
- **Bandwidth Conservation:** Edge deployment reduces the amount of data that needs to be transmitted over the network, saving bandwidth and reducing costs.

Common Edge Deployment Options:

- **Mobile Phones:**
    - *Core ML (iOS):* Apple's framework for deploying machine learning models on iOS devices.
    - *TensorFlow Lite (Android):* Google's framework for deploying machine learning models on Android devices.
    - *PyTorch Mobile (iOS and Android):* Allows you to run PyTorch models directly on mobile devices.
- **IoT Devices:**
    - *TensorFlow Lite Micro:* A lightweight version of TensorFlow Lite designed for microcontrollers and other resource-constrained devices.
- **Edge Servers:**
    - *NVIDIA Jetson:* A family of embedded computing platforms designed for AI and edge computing.

Choosing the Right Platform: A Comparative Analysis

The best deployment platform for your specific application will depend on several factors, including:

- **Latency Requirements:** If you need low latency, edge deployment is the better option.
- **Scalability Requirements:** If you need high scalability, cloud deployment is the better option.
- **Privacy Requirements:** If you need to protect sensitive data, edge deployment is the better option.
- **Cost Constraints:** Cloud platforms offer pay-as-you-go pricing, but edge deployment may be more cost-effective in the long run for high-volume applications.
- **Accessibility Requirements:** If you need to make your model accessible to users from anywhere in the world, cloud deployment is the better option.
- **Skillset:** What frameworks and tools is your team familiar with.

Personal Insight: The best approach might be a combination of both cloud and edge deployment, such as using the cloud for training and model management and deploying the model to the edge for inference.

Conclusion

Choosing the right deployment platform is a critical step in bringing your PyTorch models to life and solving real-world problems. By understanding the trade-offs between cloud and edge deployment, you can select the platform that best meets the needs of your specific application. Now, it is time to take your work to the real world!

Chapter 12: Performance Optimization with torch.compile - Unleashing the Speed Demon Within

In the world of deep learning, speed is paramount. Whether you're training massive models or deploying them to real-time applications, performance optimization is crucial for achieving your goals. PyTorch 2.0 introduced a game-changing feature called torch.compile (powered by Dynamo) that simplifies the process of optimizing your PyTorch code for speed. This chapter will be your guide to mastering torch.compile and unlocking the full performance potential of your PyTorch models. Think of this as learning to tune a high-performance engine to achieve maximum speed and efficiency.

Why torch.compile Matters: torch.compile allows you to:

- **Boost Performance with Minimal Code Changes:** Often, you can achieve significant speedups with just a single line of code.
- **Automate Optimization:** torch.compile automatically applies a variety of optimization techniques, freeing you from manually tuning low-level details.
- **Target Different Hardware:** torch.compile can be used to optimize your code for different hardware platforms, including CPUs and GPUs.

12.1 Introduction to torch.compile (Dynamo) - A New Era of PyTorch Performance: The One-Line Speed Boost

In the ever-evolving landscape of deep learning, the quest for faster training and inference is a constant pursuit. PyTorch 2.0 arrived with a game-changing feature designed to address this very need: torch.compile. It's not just an incremental improvement, but a paradigm shift that unlocks a new era of PyTorch performance with minimal code changes. Think of it as swapping out your engine for a high-performance model – instantly boosting your speed and efficiency.

Why torch.compile Matters: This simple yet powerful function allows you to:

- **Achieve Significant Speedups:** Often, you can observe substantial performance improvements with a single line of code.
- **Automate Optimization:** torch.compile intelligently applies various optimization techniques under the hood, saving you the hassle of manual tuning.
- **Empower Hardware Acceleration:** It works hand-in-hand with hardware accelerators (GPUs, TPUs) to maximize their utilization.

Dynamo: The Engine Behind the Magic

Under the hood, torch.compile is powered by a new technology called Dynamo. Dynamo acts as a *dynamic tracing compiler*, meaning that it observes your PyTorch code at runtime and then transforms it into a more efficient representation. This allows it to optimize your code specifically for the operations you're performing, without requiring you to change your code manually.

Key Concepts:

- **Dynamic Tracing:** Observing the execution of your PyTorch code at runtime to understand the operations being performed.
- **Graph Representation:** Converting the observed operations into a graph data structure that represents the flow of data through your model.
- **Backend Compilation:** Using a backend compiler (like torch._dynamo.optimize with backends such as eager, nvfuser, aot_autograd and inductor) to generate optimized code based on the graph representation.

The Transformation Process:

1. **Wrap with torch.compile:** You simply wrap your model or function with torch.compile.
2. **Dynamic Observation:** When you run the compiled code, Dynamo dynamically observes the operations being performed.
3. **Graph Creation:** Dynamo constructs a graph representation of these operations, capturing the flow of data.
4. **Backend Compilation:** Dynamo then leverages a backend compiler (like TorchInductor) to generate optimized code tailored to the observed operations.
5. **Execution:** Finally, the optimized code is executed, resulting in a noticeable performance boost.

Practical Example:

Let's say you have a simple neural network model:

```python
import torch
import torch.nn as nn

# Define a simple neural network
class MyModel(nn.Module):
    def __init__(self):
        super().__init__()
        self.linear1 = nn.Linear(10, 20)
        self.relu = nn.ReLU()
        self.linear2 = nn.Linear(20, 5)

    def forward(self, x):
        x = self.linear1(x)
        x = self.relu(x)
        x = self.linear2(x)
        return x
```

To compile it using torch.compile, you simply add one line of code:

```python
import torch
import torch.nn as nn

# Define a simple neural network
class MyModel(nn.Module):
    def __init__(self):
        super().__init__()
        self.linear1 = nn.Linear(10, 20)
        self.relu = nn.ReLU()
        self.linear2 = nn.Linear(20, 5)

    def forward(self, x):
        x = self.linear1(x)
        x = self.relu(x)
        x = self.linear2(x)
        return x

# 1. Create an instance of the model
model = MyModel()

# 2. COMPILE!
compiled_model = torch.compile(model)  #Now you can use this
to train and infer!
```

```
# 3. Training and inference as usual - use compiled_model
instead of model!
# (Rest of your training/inference code would go here)
```

Key Notes:

- torch.compile is designed to be a drop-in replacement for your existing models. You can simply replace model with compiled_model in your training and inference code.
- It works best for large models and complex operations where the compilation overhead is amortized over many iterations.
- It may not be able to improve performance, or even hurt performance, in rare cases.

Practical Implementation Notes:

- The first time a function is called, torch.compile will compile it. Subsequent runs of the function will execute faster due to the cached compiled code.
- Make sure to use it on more significant networks, as it may hurt the performance in smaller networks!

Personal Insight: The speed and ease of torch.compile is fantastic. Now, I benchmark my code before and after using it in order to make a fair comparison and make sure the code is faster!

Conclusion

torch.compile marks a new era of PyTorch performance, offering a remarkably simple way to optimize your models for speed and efficiency. Dynamo, the engine behind torch.compile, is an important framework. If you do not have it, make sure to upgrade your PyTorch! By understanding the principles of dynamic tracing and graph compilation, you can effectively leverage torch.compile to unleash the speed demon within your PyTorch code. Now, let's compare and see how it compares to our current implementation!

12.2 Benchmarking Performance Gains - Measuring the Speed Boost: Seeing is Believing

While torch.compile promises significant performance improvements, it's crucial to *quantify* those gains through careful benchmarking. Benchmarking allows you to measure the actual speedup achieved by torch.compile on your specific model and hardware, helping you to make informed decisions about its effectiveness. Think of this as running a dyno test on your newly tuned engine – confirming that all the effort has paid off.

Why Benchmarking Matters: Benchmarking provides:

- **Quantifiable Evidence:** Hard numbers to prove the performance benefits of torch.compile.
- **Identification of Bottlenecks:** Insights into which parts of your code are benefiting the most (or least) from compilation.
- **Confidence in Deployment:** Assurance that your optimized model will perform as expected in production.

The torch.utils.benchmark Module: Your Benchmarking Toolkit

PyTorch provides a built-in module called torch.utils.benchmark that makes it easy to measure the execution time of your code. This module offers a convenient way to compare the performance of different implementations or configurations.

Key Features:

- **Timer Class:** The core class for measuring execution time.
- **timeit Method:** Runs the code multiple times and returns the average execution time.
- **compare Function:** Compares the performance of multiple implementations and generates a detailed report.

Best Practices For Fair Benchmarks:

- Do NOT benchmark a model after it is compiled for the first time. Wait for the cache to be loaded.
- Set up CUDA properly by warming it up.

- Do not rely on just one run, as there are many background tasks occurring. It is better to run and use the .timeit() call, where the program is run multiple times.

Let's see how to use torch.utils.benchmark to measure the performance gains of torch.compile:

```python
    import torch
import torch.nn as nn
import torch.utils.benchmark as benchmark

# 1. Define a Model (example)
class SimpleNet(nn.Module): #Same model, as before.
    def __init__(self, input_size, hidden_size, output_size):
        super(SimpleNet, self).__init__()
        self.fc1 = nn.Linear(input_size, hidden_size)
        self.relu = nn.ReLU()
        self.fc2 = nn.Linear(hidden_size, output_size)

    def forward(self, x):
        x = self.fc1(x)
        x = self.relu(x)
        x = self.fc2(x)
        return x

# 2. Instantiate the Model
input_size = 10
hidden_size = 5
output_size = 1
model = SimpleNet(input_size, hidden_size, output_size)

# 3. Create Sample Input - Example to run test
example = torch.rand(1024, input_size) #Set the right batch.

# First, warm up CUDA.
model(example)
compiled_model = torch.compile(model)
compiled_model(example)

#Benchmark without compilation.
baseResult = benchmark.Timer(
    stmt='model(example)',
    setup='from __main__ import model, example',
    globals={'model':model, 'example':example})

#Benchmark the compiled model
compileResult = benchmark.Timer(
    stmt='compiled_model(example)',
    setup='from __main__ import compiled_model, example',
```

```
    globals={'compiled_model':compiled_model,
'example':example})

#Check Speedups (in order!) - run 10 times.
print("Base:")
print(baseResult.timeit(10))
print("Compiled")
print(compileResult.timeit(10))
```

Understanding the Code:

- We create a Timer object for both the original model and the compiled model, with different names.
- We use the timeit method to run each implementation multiple times (10 iterations in this case) and measure the average execution time.

Important Notes:

- The benchmarking process includes "warming up" the code by running it once before starting the timer. This helps to avoid measuring the overhead of the first execution. We run each one of them.

Personal Insight: I've found that benchmarking is crucial for understanding the true impact of torch.compile. In some cases, I've been surprised to see that torch.compile actually *decreased* performance for certain small models. This highlights the importance of measuring the performance on your specific code and hardware. If this occurs, do NOT use.

Beyond torch.utils.benchmark: More Detailed Profiling

For more in-depth analysis of your code's performance, you can use profiling tools like torch.profiler. This tool allows you to identify performance bottlenecks and see how much time is being spent in different parts of your code.

Conclusion

Benchmarking is essential for understanding the performance gains achieved by torch.compile. By using the torch.utils.benchmark module and profiling tools, you can quantify the speedups, identify bottlenecks, and ensure that your optimized code is performing as expected. Always test the results! In our next section, we will be addressing what the modes are.

12.3 Understanding mode Options and Trade-offs - Fine-Tuning the Optimization: Dialing in the Perfect Settings

torch.compile is not a one-size-fits-all solution. To provide more granularity, it has several mode options. While torch.compile is remarkably easy to use, it also offers a degree of fine-grained control through its "mode" options. These modes allow you to tailor the optimization process to your specific needs, balancing compilation time with runtime performance. Think of this as adjusting the settings on your high-performance engine – tweaking the air-fuel mixture, ignition timing, and turbo boost to achieve the perfect balance of power and efficiency.

Why Mode Options Matter: Understanding mode options allows you to:

- Optimize for different deployment scenarios (e.g., training vs. inference).
- Balance compilation time with runtime performance.
- Target specific hardware platforms.

Exploring the mode Options: A Detailed Overview

torch.compile offers several built-in mode options, each with its own strengths and weaknesses:

- **default:** This is the default mode and provides a good balance between compilation time and runtime performance. It applies a set of common optimization techniques that are generally effective for a wide range of models. This is a good starting point when optimizing.
- **reduce-overhead:** This mode prioritizes reducing framework overhead, which can be beneficial for latency-sensitive applications. It may result in longer compilation times. It's meant for use cases when "hiccups" may lead to significant impact.
- **max-autotune:** This mode performs extensive autotuning to find the best optimization strategy for your code. Autotuning involves trying out different compilation configurations and measuring their performance to identify the optimal settings. This mode can achieve the highest runtime performance but also has the longest compilation time.

Understanding the Trade-offs:

The key trade-off between these modes is between *compilation time* and *runtime performance.*

- default offers a good balance, with reasonable compilation times and decent performance gains.
- reduce-overhead prioritizes low latency, potentially at the cost of slightly longer compilation times or reduced peak performance.
- max-autotune prioritizes maximum runtime performance, accepting potentially very long compilation times.

Implementation: Specifying the mode Option

To specify the mode option, you simply pass it as an argument to the torch.compile function:

```
import torch
import torch.nn as nn
import torch.utils.benchmark as benchmark

# 1. Define a Model (example)
class SimpleNet(nn.Module): #Same model, as before.
    def __init__(self, input_size, hidden_size, output_size):
        super(SimpleNet, self).__init__()
        self.fc1 = nn.Linear(input_size, hidden_size)
        self.relu = nn.ReLU()
        self.fc2 = nn.Linear(hidden_size, output_size)

    def forward(self, x):
        x = self.fc1(x)
        x = self.relu(x)
        x = self.fc2(x)
        return x

# 2. Instantiate the Model
input_size = 10
hidden_size = 5
output_size = 1
model = SimpleNet(input_size, hidden_size, output_size)

# 3. Create Sample Input - Example to run test
example = torch.rand(1024, input_size)

#Benchmark different modes
defaultResult = benchmark.Timer(
    stmt='model(example)',
```

```
    setup='from __main__ import model, example, torch',
    globals={'model': torch.compile(model, mode="default"),
'example':example})
reduceOverheadResult = benchmark.Timer(
    stmt='model(example)',
    setup='from __main__ import model, example, torch',
    globals={'model': torch.compile(model, mode="reduce-
overhead"), 'example':example})
maxAutotuneResult = benchmark.Timer(
    stmt='model(example)',
    setup='from __main__ import model, example, torch',
    globals={'model': torch.compile(model, mode="max-
autotune"), 'example':example})

#Check Speedups (in order!)
print("Default Mode, lower is better")
print(defaultResult.timeit(10))
print("Reduce-Overhead Mode, lower is better")
print(reduceOverheadResult.timeit(10))
print("Max-Autotune Mode, lower is better")
print(maxAutotuneResult.timeit(10))
```

When to Use Which Mode: A Practical Guide

- **default:** Use this mode as a starting point for most applications. It provides a good balance of compilation time and runtime performance.
- **reduce-overhead:** Consider this mode when you need to minimize the framework overhead and are willing to potentially sacrifice some peak performance. This is best used in production-oriented applications.
- **max-autotune:** Use this mode when you need the absolute best runtime performance and are willing to wait for the autotuning process to complete. This is useful in deployment scenarios or specific research projects.

Personal Insight: I usually start with the default mode and then experiment with the other modes if I need to further optimize performance. The choice depends heavily on the size of your network and the time it takes to train.

Conclusion

Understanding the mode options in torch.compile allows you to fine-tune the optimization process to your specific needs, balancing compilation time with runtime performance. This fine-tuning enables your models to be much more efficient. Great work! Now, let's troubleshoot some of the problems that may occur.

12.4 Troubleshooting and Best Practices for torch.compile - Navigating the Optimization Landscape: Taming the Beast

While torch.compile is designed to be user-friendly, the reality is that you might encounter some bumps along the road. As a new and evolving technology, it's not always a seamless experience. This section is your guide to navigating the optimization landscape, troubleshooting common issues, and adopting best practices for using torch.compile effectively. Think of this as learning how to diagnose and repair your high-performance engine – understanding the common problems and the techniques for resolving them.

Why Troubleshooting and Best Practices Matter: Understanding these issues allows you to:

- Overcome common obstacles to successful compilation.
- Identify and resolve performance regressions.
- Write code that is more compatible with torch.compile.
- Contribute to the ongoing development of torch.compile.

Common Issues and Solutions: A Troubleshooting Guide

Let's delve into some common problems you might encounter when using torch.compile and their potential solutions:

- **Incompatibilities with Certain Operations:**
  - *Problem:* Some PyTorch operations may not be fully supported by torch.compile. This can result in errors during the compilation process or unexpected behavior at runtime.
  - *Solution:*
    1. Check Compatibility: Consult the PyTorch documentation and community forums to see if the operation is known to be incompatible.
    2. Rewrite Code: Try rewriting your code to use more basic or alternative operations that are known to be compatible. For example, replace custom functions with equivalent PyTorch built-in functions.

3. Conditional Compilation: Use torch._dynamo.config.suppress(condition) to selectively disable compilation for specific parts of your code.

- **Dynamic Control Flow:**
  - o *Problem:* Models with complex control flow that depends on the input data (e.g., if statements or while loops) can be difficult to compile effectively with torch.compile.
  - o *Solution:*
    1. Use Scripting: Convert your model to TorchScript using the @torch.jit.script decorator to handle control flow.
    2. Simplify Control Flow: Try to simplify the control flow in your code to make it easier for torch.compile to analyze and optimize.

- **Long Compilation Times:**
  - o *Problem:* The compilation process can take a significant amount of time, especially for large models.
  - o *Solution:*
    1. Use default Mode: Start with the default mode, which offers a good balance between compilation time and runtime performance.
    2. Reduce Model Size: If possible, try reducing the size of your model by removing unnecessary layers or parameters.
    3. Cache Compilation Results: torch.compile caches the results of the compilation process, so subsequent runs will be faster. To ensure proper caching, you have to call the model more than once.
    4. Upgrade your CPU/RAM.

- **Unexpected Errors or Crashes:**
  - o *Problem:* torch.compile is a relatively new feature, and you may encounter unexpected errors or crashes.
  - o *Solution:*
    1. Check PyTorch Version: Ensure that you are using the latest version of PyTorch.
    2. Report the Issue: Report the issue to the PyTorch developers, providing a minimal reproducible example.

- **Performance Regressions:**
  - o *Problem:* In some cases, torch.compile may actually *decrease* the performance of your code.

- Solution:
    1. Benchmark Carefully: Always benchmark your code before and after using torch.compile to ensure that you are actually seeing a performance improvement.
    2. Try Different Modes: Experiment with different mode options to see if you can find a configuration that performs better. If not, disable TorchCompile.
    3. Report the Issue: Report the performance regression to the PyTorch developers, providing a minimal reproducible example.

Known Incompatibilities:

- torch.compile and CUDA Graphs are not currently compatible.
- Dynamic shapes that change per iteration

Personal Insight: I've encountered a few cases where torch.compile actually *slowed down* my code. In those cases, I simply disabled torch.compile and moved on. The key is to always measure and verify.

Best Practices for Using torch.compile: A Checklist for Success

To maximize your chances of success with torch.compile, follow these best practices:

- **Start Simple:** Begin by compiling small sections of your code to identify any potential issues early on.
- **Test Thoroughly:** Test your code after compiling it to ensure that it's working correctly. Pay attention to any changes in behavior or accuracy.
- **Benchmark Carefully:** Use benchmarking tools to measure the performance of your code before and after compilation.
- **Profile Your Code:** Use profiling tools to identify performance bottlenecks and focus your optimization efforts on the most critical areas.
- **Check for Updates:** Stay up-to-date with the latest PyTorch releases and documentation to take advantage of new features and bug fixes.
- **Contribute to the Community:** Report any issues or performance regressions that you encounter to the PyTorch developers.

Code Example: Conditionally Disabling Compilation

As described in the troubleshooting code block, let's show the proper approach:

```
import torch

#Function for conditional compilation.
@torch._dynamo.config.patch(dynamic_shapes=False)
def useModel (model, item):
  return model(item) #Run this particular model

#Check code, works, then remove comments!
```

Conclusion

torch.compile is a powerful tool, but it's important to approach it with a healthy dose of caution and a willingness to troubleshoot potential issues. By following the troubleshooting tips and best practices outlined in this chapter, you can effectively navigate the optimization landscape and unlock the full performance potential of your PyTorch models. Congrats! You can now fine tune and solve common problems! This is the end of our book, let me know what else I can do!

Chapter 13: Quantization and Pruning - Slimming Down and Speeding Up Your Models

In the pursuit of efficient deep learning, it's not enough to just train accurate models – you also need to make them small and fast enough to deploy on resource-constrained devices or to handle high-throughput inference. This chapter explores two powerful techniques for reducing model size and improving inference speed: quantization and pruning. We'll also touch on hardware acceleration, which can further boost performance. Think of this chapter as learning to be a minimalist architect, designing elegant and efficient structures with only the essential components.

Why Quantization and Pruning Matter: These techniques allow you to:

- Reduce model size, making them easier to deploy on mobile devices, embedded systems, and other resource-constrained platforms.
- Improve inference speed, enabling faster predictions and lower latency.
- Reduce energy consumption, making your models more environmentally friendly.

13.1 Model Quantization Techniques - From Floating-Point to Integer: Trimming the Fat - Squeezing More Performance From Less

In the quest for efficient deep learning, the pursuit of smaller and faster models is a constant endeavor. While powerful, neural networks can be resource-intensive, particularly when deployed on edge devices or in high-throughput scenarios. Model quantization is a transformative technique that addresses this challenge by reducing the precision of a neural network's weights and activations, resulting in smaller model sizes and improved inference speeds. Think of it as slimming down a recipe by substituting ingredients, you can achieve a similar flavor profile with a fraction of the calories.

Why Model Quantization Matters: Quantization enables:

- **Reduced Model Size:** Smaller models require less storage space and bandwidth, making them easier to deploy on resource-constrained devices.
- **Improved Inference Speed:** Integer operations are generally faster than floating-point operations, leading to faster inference times.
- **Lower Power Consumption:** Reduced memory access and faster computations can lead to lower power consumption, extending battery life on mobile devices.

Understanding the Fundamentals: Floating-Point vs. Integer Precision

The core idea behind quantization is to represent the weights and activations of a neural network using lower-precision data types. By default, PyTorch uses 32-bit floating-point numbers (float32) to represent these values. Quantization involves converting these values to lower-precision formats, such as 8-bit integers (int8) or even lower.

- **Floating-Point Precision:** Offers a wide range of values and high precision, but requires more storage space and computational resources.
- **Integer Precision:** Offers a smaller range of values and lower precision, but requires less storage space and is faster to compute.

Practical Examples:

- A float32 number requires 4 bytes of storage, while an int8 number requires only 1 byte.
- Integer arithmetic is generally faster than floating-point arithmetic on most hardware platforms.

Types of Quantization: Choosing the Right Approach

There are several different approaches to quantization, each with its own trade-offs between accuracy and performance. The appropriate type of quantization to use will depend on the specific requirements of your application.

- **Dynamic Quantization:** In dynamic quantization, the scaling factor and zero point are calculated dynamically for each batch of data. This approach is relatively simple to implement and doesn't require any training data, but it can be less accurate than other methods. This is also used for LSTM and RNN model types.

- **Static Quantization:** Also known as post-training quantization (PTQ), static quantization involves calibrating the model with a representative dataset to determine the optimal scaling factors and zero points for each layer. This approach typically provides better accuracy than dynamic quantization.
- **Quantization-Aware Training (QAT):** This is the most advanced approach to quantization. QAT involves training the model with quantization in mind, simulating the effects of quantization during training to improve the model's robustness to the lower-precision data types. It typically provides the best accuracy, but it requires more effort to implement. It helps "learn" the right values under the quantization constraints.

Dynamic Quantization: The Easiest Path to Optimization

Dynamic quantization is the simplest form of quantization to implement and is a good starting point. It converts the weights to int8 but leaves the activations as float32. Because it quantizes dynamically, no calibration is required.

Key Steps:

1. Convert the model's weights to int8.
2. Convert certain operations, such as Linear and RNN to also run using quantization.
3. Run the model as it is.

```
    import torch
import torch.nn as nn

#Quantizing Dynamically is easier.
#Must quantize the Linear and RNN modules, otherwise won't
work.
model_fp32 = nn.Sequential(
    nn.Linear(10, 10),
    nn.ReLU(),
    nn.Linear(10, 1)
)
model_quantized = torch.quantization.quantize_dynamic(
    model_fp32, {torch.nn.Linear, torch.nn.LSTM,
torch.nn.GRU}, dtype=torch.qint8
)
print(model_quantized)

#Test Results - Check the weights and biases to ensure
```

```
example = torch.randn(1, 10)
res = model_quantized(example)
print(res) #Check
```

Static Quantization: Better Accuracy with Calibration

Static quantization, also known as post-training quantization (PTQ), offers a better trade-off between accuracy and performance. It requires a calibration step, where you run a representative dataset through the model to collect statistics about the range of values for the activations. These statistics are then used to determine the optimal scaling factors and zero points for each layer.

```
import torch
import torch.nn as nn
import torch.quantization

# 1. Define a Model (example) - Need to set `quantize = True`
in the config.
class SimpleNet(nn.Module):
    def __init__(self, input_size, hidden_size, output_size):
        super(SimpleNet, self).__init__()
        self.fc1 = nn.Linear(input_size, hidden_size)
        self.relu = nn.ReLU()
        self.fc2 = nn.Linear(hidden_size, output_size)

    def forward(self, x):
        x = self.fc1(x)
        x = self.relu(x)
        x = self.fc2(x)
        return x

# 2. Instantiate the Model
input_size = 10
hidden_size = 5
output_size = 1
model_fp32 = SimpleNet(input_size, hidden_size, output_size)
#FP32 Model.
model_fp32.eval() # Must call eval()

#Attach a qconfig for what you want to measure.
model_fp32.qconfig =
torch.quantization.get_default_qconfig('fbgemm') #Or any
other config you want to try.

#Push down the configurations to the model:
model_prepared = torch.quantization.prepare(model_fp32) #Or
prepare_fx
```

```
# calibrate model to determine ranges - you will need a data
input process here!
# It needs to have seen what the real distributions look
like!
exampleInput = torch.randn(1, input_size)
model_prepared(exampleInput)

# convert
model_int8 = torch.quantization.convert(model_prepared)

#Verify
print("The layers you quantized, if any: ",model_int8)

# 6. Example and result
example = torch.randn(1, input_size)
res = model_int8(example)
print(res)
```

Key steps:

1. Preparation: Set configurations to apply to the model.
2. Calibration: This step is crucial. The model observes data from your inputs.
3. Conversion: Model layers are then quantized.

Implementation Notes:

- The choice of qconfig will depend on the hardware platform where you intend to deploy the model.
- The calibration dataset should be representative of the data that the model will encounter in production.

Personal Insight: I've found that static quantization generally provides a better trade-off between accuracy and performance than dynamic quantization. The calibration step is essential for achieving good accuracy with static quantization.

Quantization Aware Training: Maximizing Accuracy with Training

Quantization-aware training (QAT) is the most advanced approach to quantization. It involves training the model with quantization in mind, simulating the effects of quantization during training to improve the model's robustness to the lower-precision data types.

Key Steps:

1. Prepare: Set model configurations
2. Training: Train the model using forward and backward passes to fine tune the model with the quantization
3. Convert: Convert the model using the convert step.

Conclusion

Model quantization is a powerful technique for reducing the size of neural networks and improving their inference speed. By understanding the different quantization approaches and how to implement them in PyTorch, you can effectively optimize your models for deployment on resource-constrained platforms. You have now slimmed down and trimmed the fat, you have created the most efficient model possible!

13.2 Pruning: Reducing Model Size and Complexity - Trimming the Unnecessary: Sculpting Leaner, Faster Networks

In the world of deep learning, less is often more. While large, over-parameterized models can achieve impressive accuracy, they can also be computationally expensive and difficult to deploy on resource-constrained devices. Pruning is a powerful technique for addressing this challenge by selectively removing connections (weights) that are deemed unimportant, resulting in smaller, faster, and more efficient models. Think of it as sculpting a statue – chipping away the excess material to reveal the essential form.

Why Pruning Matters: Pruning allows you to:

- **Reduce Model Size:** Smaller models require less storage space and bandwidth.
- **Improve Inference Speed:** Fewer connections lead to faster computations.
- **Reduce Energy Consumption:** Less computation translates to lower power usage, particularly important for mobile and edge deployments.

Understanding Sparsity: The Goal of Pruning

The primary goal of pruning is to increase the *sparsity* of a neural network. Sparsity refers to the percentage of weights that are set to zero. A higher sparsity means that the model has fewer non-zero connections, resulting in a smaller and faster model.

Methods for Pruning: Choosing the Right Approach

There are several different methods for pruning a neural network, each with its own trade-offs between accuracy and performance:

- **Unstructured Pruning:** This method involves removing individual weights from the network. It's the most flexible approach and can achieve high sparsity levels, but it can be difficult to implement efficiently on some hardware platforms.
- **Structured Pruning:** This method involves removing entire filters or channels from the network. It's less flexible than unstructured pruning but can be easier to implement efficiently.
- **Weight Magnitude Pruning:** A simple and widely used technique that involves removing weights with the smallest absolute values.

Pruning Strategies:

- **Global Pruning:** Pruning weights across the entire network. This is the approach used in the code example below.
- **Local Pruning:** Pruning weights within individual layers.

One-shot pruning versus iterative pruning:

- Pruning can be done all at once (one-shot pruning).
- Can also be done iteratively (prune, retrain, prune, etc.) for better performance.

Implementing Pruning in PyTorch: A Hands-On Approach

PyTorch provides a convenient set of tools for implementing pruning. Let's see how it works in practice:

```
import torch
import torch.nn as nn
import torch.nn.utils.prune as prune

# 1. Define a Model (example) - same as before!
class SimpleNet(nn.Module):
```

```python
    def __init__(self, input_size, hidden_size, output_size):
        super(SimpleNet, self).__init__()
        self.fc1 = nn.Linear(input_size, hidden_size)
        self.relu = nn.ReLU()
        self.fc2 = nn.Linear(hidden_size, output_size)

    def forward(self, x):
        x = self.fc1(x)
        x = self.relu(x)
        x = self.fc2(x)
        return x

# 2. Instantiate the Model
input_size = 10
hidden_size = 5
output_size = 1
model = SimpleNet(input_size, hidden_size, output_size)

#Parameters to prune
parameters_to_prune = (
    (model.fc1, 'weight'),
    (model.fc2, 'weight'),
)
#Prune!
prune.global_unstructured(
    parameters_to_prune,
    pruning_method=prune.L1Unstructured, #L1 Norm is used to
calculate what parameters to remove.
    amount=0.2, #Prune 20% of it.
)

#3. Check and Verify

#Iterate and show results!
for module, name in parameters_to_prune:
    print(module)
    print(list(module.named_parameters()))

example = torch.randn(1, 10) #Example dimension that has to
work with.
res = model(example)
print("Check the results, run inference and see! If it works,
perfect! ")
print(res)

#To make the prune permanent, you can run this function!
#prune.remove(model.fc1, 'weight')
```

Key Steps:

1. Define the parameters that you want to prune: You must tell it what it needs to prune!
2. Apply the pruning function: The code will take a look at the weights and prune based on your specified dimensions.
3. Verify.

Implementation Notes:

- The pruning function is not automatically applied on your model. You must use the remove function!
- You can specify the amount parameter as either a fraction (between 0 and 1) or an absolute number of weights to prune.

Personal Insight: In particular, if you have code that uses convolutions, that's where using structural pruning can be especially helpful.

Conclusion

Pruning is a powerful technique for reducing the size and complexity of your PyTorch models, making them more efficient and deployable. By understanding the different pruning methods and how to implement them, you can effectively slim down your networks and achieve optimal performance in your specific deployment environment. These techniques can be very important when you do not have access to hardware acceleration.

13.3 Hardware Acceleration (GPU/TPU) - Supercharging Your Models: Unleashing Peak Performance

While quantization and pruning help to make your models smaller and more efficient, hardware acceleration takes performance to the next level by leveraging specialized hardware designed for deep learning computations. GPUs (Graphics Processing Units) and TPUs (Tensor Processing Units) are powerful accelerators that can significantly speed up both training and inference, enabling you to tackle larger models and more complex tasks. Think of it as upgrading from a standard car to a race car – suddenly, you have access to much more power and speed.

Why Hardware Acceleration Matters:

- **Faster Training:** GPUs and TPUs can significantly reduce the training time for deep learning models, allowing you to experiment more quickly and iterate on your designs.
- **Improved Inference Speed:** Hardware acceleration can enable real-time or near-real-time inference, making your models more responsive and useful for time-sensitive applications.
- **Larger Models:** GPUs and TPUs have more memory than CPUs, allowing you to train and deploy larger models.

GPUs: The Workhorse of Deep Learning

GPUs are specialized processors that were originally designed for accelerating graphics rendering. However, their parallel architecture makes them well-suited for performing the matrix operations that are common in neural networks. GPUs have become the workhorse of deep learning, used for both training and inference.

Key Advantages of GPUs:

- **Parallel Architecture:** GPUs have hundreds or thousands of cores, allowing them to perform many operations simultaneously.
- **High Memory Bandwidth:** GPUs have high memory bandwidth, which allows them to quickly transfer data between memory and the processing cores.
- **Software Support:** PyTorch and other deep learning frameworks provide excellent support for GPUs, making it easy to move your code to the GPU and take advantage of its parallel processing capabilities.

Leveraging GPUs in PyTorch:

```python
import torch

# Check if CUDA is available
if torch.cuda.is_available():
    device = torch.device("cuda")   # Use "cuda:0" for the
first GPU, "cuda:1" for the second, etc.
    print("CUDA is available. Using GPU.")
else:
    device = torch.device("cpu")
    print("CUDA is not available. Using CPU.")

# Move your model and data to the GPU
#Move Model to appropriate location
```

```
model = model.to(device)

#Move data to appropriate location
data = data.to(device)
labels = labels.to(device)

#Perform Training / Inferance:
#Example Run
example = torch.randn(1, 10).to(device)
res = model(example)
print(res) #Show result.
```

Best Practices for Using GPUs:

- **Use CUDA:** Make sure you have a CUDA-enabled GPU and the appropriate drivers installed.
- **Check for Availability:** Use torch.cuda.is_available() to check if CUDA is available before attempting to move your model and data to the GPU.
- **Move Data and Model:** Use model.to(device) and data.to(device) to move your model and data to the GPU.
- **Use Data Parallelism:** Use torch.nn.DataParallel to distribute the training workload across multiple GPUs. Make sure to perform the appropriate transforms as well!
- **Monitor GPU Usage:** Monitor the GPU usage during training to ensure that the GPU is being fully utilized.

Personal Insight: Moving my code to the GPU was one of the biggest performance boosts I ever experienced. It allowed me to train much larger models and experiment more quickly.

TPUs: Google's Custom-Designed Accelerator

TPUs are custom-designed hardware accelerators developed by Google specifically for deep learning. They are optimized for performing the matrix operations that are common in neural networks and can provide significant performance improvements over GPUs for certain types of models.

Key Advantages of TPUs:

- **High Computational Throughput:** TPUs are designed for high-throughput matrix operations.

- **Large Memory Capacity:** TPUs have a large amount of on-chip memory, which allows them to store the entire model and dataset in memory.
- **Interconnect Optimization:** Optimized for communication and high throughput.

Using TPUs with PyTorch:

While PyTorch has traditionally had less direct integration with TPUs compared to TensorFlow, recent efforts have made it easier to utilize TPUs. Google Cloud TPUs often require using specific libraries and APIs, so check the Google Cloud documentation. Pytorch also has some preliminary support for it.

To run on TPU, these are the basic changes to the code:

```
    #To use TPU
import torch_xla.core.xla_model as xm

#Use xm.xla_device() for devices
device = xm.xla_device()

#Have this line as part of parallel training.
xm.optimizer_step(optimizer, barrier=True)
```

Key Considerations for Using TPUs:

- Check compatibility, may need a model rewrite.
- Use the correct CUDA driver!

Choosing the Right Accelerator: A Summary

- *GPUs:*
  - **Pros:** Widely available, excellent software support, versatile for a wide range of tasks.
  - **Cons:** More expensive than CPUs, require a compatible system.
- *TPUs:*
  - **Pros:** Excellent computational throughput, optimized for deep learning.
  - **Cons:** Only available on Google Cloud, require code modifications, less versatile than GPUs.

Personal Insight: Cloud TPUs are an excellent choice for large-scale training jobs, but they require more specialized knowledge to use effectively. For local development and smaller-scale projects, GPUs are often the more practical option.

Conclusion

Hardware acceleration is a crucial step in achieving optimal performance with your deep learning models. By understanding the capabilities of GPUs and TPUs and how to leverage them in PyTorch, you can significantly speed up your training and inference workflows and tackle more ambitious projects. This is often the "final step" for scaling your model, make sure to try it out!

Chapter 14: Distributed Training - Scaling Deep Learning to New Heights

As deep learning models grow ever larger and datasets become increasingly massive, the need for distributed training becomes paramount. Distributed training is the technique of splitting the training workload across multiple GPUs or machines, allowing you to train models that would be impossible to fit on a single device. This chapter is your guide to harnessing the power of distributed training, enabling you to scale your deep learning projects to new heights.

Why Distributed Training Matters: Distributed training allows you to:

- **Train Larger Models:** Train models that are too large to fit on a single GPU.
- **Reduce Training Time:** Significantly reduce the training time for large models and datasets.
- **Scale to Massive Datasets:** Train on datasets that are too large to fit in the memory of a single machine.

14.1 Data Parallelism with DistributedDataParallel - Multiplying Your Computational Power: Unleashing the Horde

Data parallelism is a cornerstone of distributed deep learning, offering a way to significantly reduce training time by distributing the workload across multiple GPUs or machines. Imagine having a team of skilled artists all working simultaneously on different sections of the same giant canvas – that's the power of data parallelism. This section dives deep into how to implement data parallelism effectively using PyTorch's DistributedDataParallel (DDP) module.

Why Data Parallelism Matters: It provides a straightforward way to:

- Train larger models than a single GPU can handle.
- Significantly reduce training time on massive datasets.
- Effectively leverage multiple GPUs on a single machine or across multiple machines.

The Essence of Data Parallelism: Divide and Conquer

At its core, data parallelism involves the following steps:

1. **Model Replication:** Replicate your PyTorch model onto each available GPU or machine. Each replica has its own set of parameters.
2. **Data Partitioning:** Divide your training dataset into mini-batches. Each GPU or machine receives a different mini-batch of data.
3. **Forward Pass:** Each model replica performs a forward pass on its assigned mini-batch, computing the loss function.
4. **Backward Pass:** Each model replica performs a backward pass to calculate the gradients of the loss function with respect to its parameters.
5. **Gradient Synchronization:** Here's where the magic happens. After calculating the gradients, all the gradients across each GPU will be averaged.
6. **Parameter Update:** Now each model replica independently updates its parameters using the synchronized gradients. This ensures that all replicas are learning in the same direction.

DistributedDataParallel (DDP): PyTorch's Data Parallelism Champion

PyTorch's DistributedDataParallel (DDP) module is a powerful and efficient tool for implementing data parallelism. It handles the complex details of communication and synchronization between processes, allowing you to focus on the core aspects of your model and training loop.

Key Advantages of DDP:

- **Automatic Gradient Synchronization:** DDP automatically synchronizes gradients across all processes, simplifying the training loop.
- **High Performance:** DDP is designed for high performance, minimizing communication overhead and maximizing GPU utilization.
- **Ease of Use:** DDP is relatively easy to use, requiring minimal code changes to your existing PyTorch training scripts.
- **Scalability:** DDP can scale to hundreds or even thousands of GPUs across multiple machines.

```
import torch
```

```python
import torch.nn as nn
import torch.optim as optim
import torch.distributed as dist
import os

def setup(rank, world_size): #Set up the different processes.
    os.environ['MASTER_ADDR'] = 'localhost'
    os.environ['MASTER_PORT'] = '12355' #Change this
depending on processes running on the PC

    # initialize the process group
    dist.init_process_group("gloo", rank=rank,
world_size=world_size)

def cleanup():
    dist.destroy_process_group() #Remove the processes.

# 1. Define a Model (example) - same as before!
class SimpleNet(nn.Module):
    def __init__(self, input_size, hidden_size, output_size):
        super(SimpleNet, self).__init__()
        self.fc1 = nn.Linear(input_size, hidden_size)
        self.relu = nn.ReLU()
        self.fc2 = nn.Linear(hidden_size, output_size)

    def forward(self, x):
        x = self.fc1(x)
        x = self.relu(x)
        x = self.fc2(x)
        return x

def train(rank, world_size):
    setup(rank, world_size)
    # 2. Instantiate the Model
    input_size = 10
    hidden_size = 5
    output_size = 1
    model = SimpleNet(input_size, hidden_size, output_size)

    #Setup cuda
    device = torch.device(f"cuda:{rank}" if
torch.cuda.is_available() else "cpu") #Important

    # 3. Move model to the right device
    model = model.to(device) #Each model copy has its own
process

    # Setup DistributedDataParallel and wrap the model
    ddp_model = nn.parallel.DistributedDataParallel(model,
device_ids=[rank]) # Each model copy has its own process
```

```
    #Define the optimizer
    optimizer = optim.SGD(ddp_model.parameters(), lr=0.01)
#Only adjust lr here!

    #Create sample input
    example = torch.randn(128, 10).to(device) #Sample
dimension that has to work with.
    output = ddp_model(example) #Test

    # 4. Clean up (remove all processes at the end.)
    cleanup()

#Must spawn - make sure you wrap with if __name__ ==
'__main__': and multi processing is imported
if __name__ == '__main__':
    import torch.multiprocessing as mp
    world_size = 4 #How many devices are you using? Set
accordingly

    mp.spawn(train, # what function to run
            args=(world_size,), #What is the size of the
model?
            nprocs=world_size, #Number of processes spawned
            join=True)
```

Walking Through The Code:

1. **Setup:** The setup() function initializes the distributed environment, setting up communication between processes. This is a key first step, and it is the first thing that needs to be set up before training.
2. **Setup cuda**: Setting CUDA allows the different processes to be aware of the CUDA, to run using CUDA.
3. **Model replication and Device Transfer:** Note that the model must be *instantiated* and moved to its assigned device within each process. It needs to be duplicated so that it works. The device variable, again, allows us to control the settings.
4. **DDP Wrapping:** The nn.parallel.DistributedDataParallel wrapper is what handles the communication and synchronization of the model parameters across the devices. Now, simply use this when training or inferring.
5. **Clean up:** Call cleanup() as the last step.

Key Considerations:

- **torch.multiprocessing:** Data parallelism needs to be spawned. Make sure all parts of the code exist there, or it won't be transferred.
- Make sure you set up the processes and cuda IDs correctly.
- There can be issues with Torch and CUDA versions when running processes. Make sure these align.

Personal Insight: Using DDP can be tricky to set up, however it also can be easily implemented with the code once everything is set. For this reason, DDP is typically used for model development, but other techniques are used for scaling and production!

Scaling Your Training Loop: Adapting for Distributed Environments

To fully leverage DDP, you'll need to make a few adjustments to your training loop:

- **Data Partitioning:** Use DistributedSampler to divide your dataset into non-overlapping subsets for each process.
- **Learning Rate Adjustment:** The effective batch size is increased by the number of processes so adjust learning rate, using lr = [base_lr] * world_size

Conclusion

Data parallelism with DistributedDataParallel is a powerful technique for scaling your PyTorch training to multiple GPUs or machines. By understanding the key concepts and following the best practices outlined in this section, you can effectively reduce training time and tackle larger models and datasets. While there are complications when it comes to the setup, DDP offers a lot of flexibility. Model parallelism offers a new way to approach the scaling.

14.2 Model Parallelism for Large Models - Dividing the Network: Conquering the Memory Barrier

While Data Parallelism replicates the entire model on each device and splits the *data*, Model Parallelism takes a different approach: it splits the *model* itself across multiple devices. This is particularly useful when dealing with extremely large models that simply cannot fit into the memory of a single GPU. Think of it as breaking down a massive building project into smaller, manageable tasks, with different teams working on different parts of the structure.

Why Model Parallelism Matters: It allows you to:

- Train models that are too large to fit on a single GPU.
- Overcome memory limitations that would otherwise prevent you from training these models.
- Scale to even larger models and datasets.

The Essence of Model Parallelism: Partitioning the Network

The core idea behind model parallelism is to divide the neural network into smaller modules, with each module residing on a different device (GPU or machine). During the forward and backward passes, data is passed sequentially through these modules, with each device performing its assigned computations.

Key Concepts:

- **Model Partitioning:** Dividing the model into smaller modules.
- **Device Mapping:** Assigning each module to a specific device.
- **Data Transfer:** Transferring data between devices as it flows through the model.

Types of Model Parallelism:

- **Layer Parallelism:** Splitting the model across layers. For example, one GPU might contain the first few layers, another GPU the middle layers, and a third GPU the final layers.
- **Tensor Parallelism:** Splitting individual layers across multiple devices. This is more complex but can be useful for very large layers.

Challenges of Model Parallelism: Synchronization and Communication

Model parallelism introduces several challenges that need to be addressed:

- **Communication Overhead:** Transferring data between devices can be a significant bottleneck, especially when the devices are connected by a slow network.

- **Load Balancing:** Ensuring that each device has a similar workload to prevent some devices from becoming idle while others are overloaded.
- **Synchronization:** Synchronizing the gradients across devices after each backward pass.

Practical Notes:

- Model Parallelism is much harder to implement than Data Parallelism
- There are not many tools available
- Debugging can also be difficult.

Pipeline Parallelism: A Refined Approach

Pipeline Parallelism addresses some of the challenges of model parallelism by overlapping the forward and backward passes of different batches of data. The basic idea is to divide the model into stages and then process different batches of data through different stages simultaneously. Think of it as an assembly line, where different workers are performing different tasks on different products at the same time.

Implementing Model Parallelism: A Conceptual Example

Unfortunately, the complexities of model parallelism mean that a general, easily copy-and-pasteable code example is difficult to provide. The best approach to take would be to use a model that has an architecture you know well. For this example, we will assume that you understand what the model does.

To implement Model Parallelism, however, there are some basic steps to follow:

Setup: Import these libraries.

```
import torch
import torch.nn as nn
```

1. Chunk Up the Network Create the network in sections. As an example, we will use just a very simple 3 layer network with ReLU. This should be changed to your respective network, by cutting it up into manageable chunks.

```
    class Part1(nn.Module):
    def __init__(self):
        super(Part1, self).__init__()
        self.net = nn.Sequential(nn.Linear(10, 5),
            nn.ReLU()) #Keep only small number of operations,
this increases throughout.
    def forward(self, x):
        return self.net(x)

class Part2(nn.Module):
    def __init__(self):
        super(Part2, self).__init__()
        self.net = nn.Sequential(nn.Linear(5, 2),
            nn.ReLU())
    def forward(self, x):
        return self.net(x)

class Part3(nn.Module):
    def __init__(self):
        super(Part3, self).__init__()
        self.net = nn.Sequential(nn.Linear(2, 1))
    def forward(self, x):
        return self.net(x)
```

2. Load to Model and Set Up Model on GPU

The following code must be set up and in one function that can be passed to multiprocessing.

```
    import torch
import torch.nn as nn

def setup(): #Put in the individual processes.
  #Setup model structure
  part1 = Part1().to('cuda:0')
  part2 = Part2().to('cuda:1')
  part3 = Part3().to('cuda:2')

  #Setup input to go from one module to the next
  inputVal = torch.randn(64, 10).to('cuda:0') #Set initial
  part1Output = part1(inputVal)

  part2Output = part2(part1Output.to('cuda:1')) #The step
that passes between GPU
  part3Output = part3(part2Output.to('cuda:2')) #The step
that passes between GPU
```

Model Notes:

219

- The different models are instantiated at the start.
- The .to('cuda:0') (or other values) sets up the right GPU.
- The value is manually transferred between the GPUs and the different processes.

Personal Insight: I've found that pipeline parallelism can be challenging to implement, but it's a powerful technique for training extremely large models. This can be best implemented by first having deep experience with a particular network architecture, so the code is easy to cut up into portions.

Tensor Parallelism: Tensor Parallelism is an alternate approach to Model Parallelism. It splits up each layer into sections to further refine distribution. This is done using special libraries, such as the one written by Microsoft.

Conclusion

Model parallelism is an essential technique for training extremely large models that cannot fit on a single device. By understanding the key concepts and challenges of model parallelism, you can effectively scale your deep learning projects and tackle the most demanding tasks. While Model Parallelism may not be commonly used, it is a great tool to have that can be easily integrated into existing code. By understanding the complexities of the network and the power of torch, it can easily be made into an advantage. Congratulations, this concludes the final technical chapter in the book! What else can I do?

14.3 Strategies for Efficient Distributed Training - Optimizing the Training Process: Maximizing Performance, Minimizing Waste

Distributed training can be a game-changer for scaling your deep learning projects, but it also introduces new challenges and complexities. Simply throwing more GPUs at the problem doesn't guarantee faster training times; you need to carefully consider various strategies to optimize the training process and minimize communication overhead. Think of this as learning to manage a large team of workers – ensuring that everyone is working efficiently, communicating effectively, and avoiding unnecessary bottlenecks.

Why Optimization Matters: Efficient distributed training allows you to:

- Achieve faster convergence and reduce overall training time.
- Maximize GPU utilization and minimize idle time.
- Effectively scale your training to larger models and datasets.
- Reduce communication overhead.

The Bottleneck: Communication Overhead

The primary bottleneck in distributed training is often the communication overhead associated with synchronizing gradients and transferring data between devices. The more communication is involved, the more it can reduce the benefits of parallelization. That means code needs to be properly refactored!

Key Strategies for Efficient Distributed Training:

- **Choosing the Right Batch Size:** The choice of batch size is critical for efficient distributed training. You need to find a balance between several factors:
    - *Device Memory Capacity:* The batch size should be small enough to fit in the memory of each GPU or machine.
    - *Communication Overhead:* Larger batch sizes reduce the frequency of gradient synchronization, which can reduce communication overhead.
    - *Statistical Efficiency:* Very large batch sizes can lead to slower convergence and reduced generalization performance.

    The rule of thumb when using data parallelism is: local batch size = global batch size / world size.

- **Gradient Accumulation:** A technique where you accumulate the gradients over multiple mini-batches before performing a parameter update. This can effectively increase the batch size without increasing the memory footprint on each device. It's like gathering up all the small adjustments needed before implementing them.
- **Optimizing Communication:** Minimizing the amount of data that needs to be communicated between devices can significantly improve performance:
    - *Use All-Reduce Operations:* Use efficient all-reduce operations provided by PyTorch's distributed communication library to synchronize gradients across all processes.
    - *Compress Gradients:* Consider compressing the gradients before sending them over the network.

- **Overlap Communication and Computation:** Hide the latency of communication by overlapping it with computation. This can be achieved using techniques like asynchronous gradient updates. You want to set it up so that your workers are always working, or communicating to other workers.

Implementation Tips for DDP: Maximizing Performance

When using DistributedDataParallel (DDP), consider the following implementation tips:

- *Launch Utilities:* Use the appropriate launch utilities (e.g., torch.distributed.launch) to start your distributed training script.
- *Barrier:* At key moments during training, use torch.distributed.barrier() to ensure that all processes are synchronized.
- *Gloo vs NCCL:* For CPUs, use Gloo, for NVIDIA GPUs use NCCL.

A "Good" Example Of Implementation:

1. First run the following using multiple GPUs with each process:

```
torchrun --nnodes 1 --nproc_per_node 4 your_script.py
```

1. Check to make sure that the setup of the rank works.
2. Run code to completion.
3. Make sure that it is performant by watching the nvidia-smi and watching that the utilization is high.

If there is a communication error, then it is most likely that this function is the issue.

```
    def setup(rank, world_size): #Set up the different
processes.
    os.environ['MASTER_ADDR'] = 'localhost'
    os.environ['MASTER_PORT'] = '12355' #Change this
depending on processes running on the PC

    # initialize the process group
    dist.init_process_group("gloo", rank=rank,
world_size=world_size)
```

Personal Insight: I've learned that efficient distributed training is not just about using more GPUs. It's about carefully optimizing the training process to minimize communication overhead and maximize GPU utilization. I find that spending time profiling my code and identifying bottlenecks is crucial for achieving good scaling.

Conclusion

Achieving efficient distributed training requires careful planning, optimization, and a deep understanding of the underlying hardware and software. By following the strategies outlined in this chapter, you can effectively scale your deep learning projects to new heights and tackle even the most demanding tasks. It is a continuous process to ensure that the efficiency is high.

You are now equipped to skillfully optimize the training process and achieve efficient distributed training in PyTorch! Congratulations again for finishing this book!

Appendix

This appendix is designed to serve as a helpful resource as you continue your journey with PyTorch. We'll cover common errors and how to fix them, as well as a selection of useful libraries and tools that can streamline your deep learning workflow.

• **Common Errors and Solutions**

Debugging is an essential part of the deep learning process. Here are some common errors you might encounter and how to address them:

1. **CUDA Out of Memory Error:**
   o **Cause:** Your model or data is too large to fit in GPU memory.
   o **Solutions:**
      ▪ Reduce batch size: Reduce the number of samples processed in each iteration.
      ▪ Use smaller models: Try a model with fewer parameters.
      ▪ Use mixed-precision training: Reduce the memory footprint of the model by using torch.float16 (half precision).
      ▪ Free up memory: Clear unused variables from memory using del and torch.cuda.empty_cache().
      ▪ Use gradient accumulation: Helps reduce the total number of parameters at once.
      ▪ Prune: Cut some of the model away to free up space.
2. **Shape Mismatch Errors:**
   o **Cause:** The dimensions of your tensors don't match the expected input shape of a layer or function.
   o **Solutions:**
      ▪ Double-check the shapes of your tensors: Use tensor.shape to inspect the dimensions of your tensors.
      ▪ Reshape your tensors: Use tensor.reshape() or tensor.view() to change the dimensions of your tensors.
      ▪ Verify Layer Definitions: Double-check the in_features and out_features parameters of your linear layers and the kernel_size and stride parameters of your convolutional layers.
3. **Type Errors:**

- o **Cause:** You're using the wrong data type for a tensor or function argument.
- o **Solutions:**
    - Check the expected data type: Consult the PyTorch documentation to see what data type is expected for each function argument.
    - Convert your tensors: Use tensor.to(dtype) to convert your tensors to the correct data type.
    - When sending to a loss function, use the right dimensions. For Cross Entropy, you need to send .long() to convert to the correct dimensions.

4. **NaN Loss:**
   - o **Cause:** The loss function is returning NaN (Not a Number) due to numerical instability, often caused by exploding gradients.
   - o **Solutions:**
       - Reduce the learning rate: A smaller learning rate can help to stabilize training.
       - Use gradient clipping: Clip the gradients to a maximum value to prevent them from exploding.
       - Use batch normalization: Batch normalization can help to stabilize the activations and gradients.
       - Use a more stable activation function: ReLU and its variants are generally more stable than sigmoid and tanh.
       - Weight Decay: helps to prevent the parameters from being too high.

5. **Model Not Learning:**
   - o **Cause:** Your model is not learning the underlying patterns in the data, resulting in poor performance.
   - o **Solutions:**
       - Check your data: Make sure your data is properly preprocessed and that the labels are correct.
       - Use a more powerful model: Try a deeper or wider architecture with more parameters.
       - Adjust your hyperparameters: Experiment with different learning rates, batch sizes, and regularization parameters.
       - Use transfer learning: Leverage pre-trained models to initialize your model with good weights.
       - Add Data Augmentation: add even more different types of data

```
# Code snippets for some of the solutions above

import torch
import torch.nn as nn

# Gradient Clipping
torch.nn.utils.clip_grad_norm_(model.parameters(),
max_norm=1) #Max Norm 1

#Data Types - Use if it is showing an error with a certain
data type.
example = torch.randn(1, 10).float()  #Force a specific type

#Move to cuda
if torch.cuda.is_available():
    device = torch.device("cuda")
    print("CUDA is available. Using GPU.")
else:
    device = torch.device("cpu")
    print("CUDA is not available. Using CPU.")

    model = model.to(device) #Load to that device.
```

Personal Insight: I've spent countless hours debugging PyTorch code over the years. The key is to be patient, methodical, and to always double-check your data, your model architecture, and your training loop.

• **Useful Libraries and Tools**

Here's a curated list of libraries and tools that can significantly enhance your PyTorch development workflow:

1. **TorchVision:** A library of pre-trained models, datasets, and image transformations for computer vision tasks.
    o Great for working with images, it has tons of different data augmentation transforms.
2. **TorchAudio:** A library for audio processing and speech recognition.
    o Similar to TorchVision, but the audio version! Great for speech and processing.
3. **TorchText:** A library for text processing and natural language understanding.
    o If you are starting to dabble with transformer models, take a look at this.
4. **Hugging Face Transformers:** A library for working with pre-trained language models like BERT, GPT, and RoBERTa.

- o Hugely useful when constructing different types of text problems, particularly classification and generation
5. **PyTorch Lightning:** A lightweight wrapper for organizing your PyTorch code, making it easier to train and deploy models.
    - o This greatly simplifies many of the training aspects with different functions!
6. **TensorBoard:** A visualization tool for monitoring your training progress, visualizing model graphs, and debugging performance issues.
    - o Great for seeing if there are any performance issues with your training. A picture is worth a thousand words
7. **Weights & Biases (W&B):** Another great platform that enables data tracking.
    - o Very good for seeing and tracking the impact of many changes.
8. **ONNX (Open Neural Network Exchange):** An open standard for representing machine learning models, allowing you to easily convert models from one framework to another.
    - o Great for running inference outside of the standard Pytorch / CUDA environments.
9. **Albumentations:** A library for fast and flexible image augmentation.
    - o This supports much more complex transformations than default PyTorch
10. **TorchServe:** Pytorch's tool to allow model deployment!
    - o This enables users to create models and push them to live using Pytorch.
11. **Torch-Pruning:** A Tool for Model Pruning.
    - o This is a great tool for seeing the impact of pruning, since it is dedicated and has all of the latest tricks!

Personal Insight: I've found that using these libraries and tools can significantly improve my productivity and the quality of my deep learning projects. Take the time to explore them and find the ones that best fit your workflow.

Conclusion

By familiarizing yourself with these common errors, their solutions, and the wealth of available libraries and tools, you'll be well-equipped to tackle the challenges of deep learning with PyTorch and to build innovative and impactful solutions. This is the conclusion of this text. All the best!

This appendix provides a solid foundation for troubleshooting and expanding your PyTorch skillset. All the best!